Educating English Language Learners in an Inclusive Environment

This book is part of the Peter Lang Education list.
Every volume is peer reviewed and meets
the highest quality standards for content and production.

PETER LANG
New York • Washington, D.C./Baltimore • Bern
Frankfurt • Berlin • Brussels • Vienna • Oxford

Youb Kim and Patricia H. Hinchey

Educating English Language Learners in an Inclusive Environment

PETER LANG
New York • Washington, D.C./Baltimore • Bern
Frankfurt • Berlin • Brussels • Vienna • Oxford

Library of Congress Cataloging-in-Publication Data

Kim, Youb.
Educating English language learners in an inclusive environment /
Youb Kim, Patricia H. Hinchey.
pages cm
Includes bibliographical references and index.
1. English language—Study and teaching—Foreign speakers.
2. Classroom environment. 3. English teachers—Training of.
I. Hinchey, Patricia H., author. II. Title.
PE1128.A2K54 428.0071—dc23 2013003330
ISBN 978-1-4331-2135-7 (hardcover)
ISBN 978-1-4331-2134-0 (paperback)
ISBN 978-1-4539-1103-7 (e-book)

Bibliographic information published by **Die Deutsche Nationalbibliothek**.
Die Deutsche Nationalbibliothek lists this publication in the "Deutsche
Nationalbibliografie"; detailed bibliographic data is available
on the Internet at http://dnb.d-nb.de/.

© 2013 Peter Lang Publishing, Inc., New York
29 Broadway, 18th floor, New York, NY 10006
www.peterlang.com

CONTENTS

FOREWORD

In their book, *Educating English Language Learners in an Inclusive Environment*, Youb Kim and Patricia Hinchey have given their teacher educator colleagues, and their teacher education candidates, a great gift—a book that is as respectful of English learners as it is insistent on deep teacher knowledge. They want to promote the development of current and future teachers who view the language and culture that English learners bring to the classroom as resources rather than instructional inconveniences. And they want those teachers to know as much as they can know about language and culture, both in general (how language and culture shape learning) and in particular (the specific affordances of the language and culture that the students in their classrooms bring with them). Why? Because that combination of respect and knowledge will lead to the development of the teaching skills they need to deliver instruction that helps students develop as effective learners in schools in which curriculum is delivered in English.

The book has all the requisite chapters and content—culture, language, literacy, assessment and pedagogy, and it is organized conveniently and convincingly. We learn first about why we should care about these issues, then about culture and language, and only then do we get to issues that embrace pedagogy explicitly. That's important and a distinctive characteristic of Kim and Hinchey's approach. Too many authors of textbooks for teachers move too soon to the practical aspects of teaching (the never-ending quest for relevance no doubt), leaving their readers knowing something about how but not why to enact certain practices. Their "first things first" commitment in those early chapters on culture and language prepares us for the pedagogical issues by grounding our understanding of teaching and learning in important linguistic and cultural concepts. The genius of the book, however, is not in its content; most books on this topic cover the same issues. Instead, its genius is in the stance the book takes toward its readers. Kim and Hinchey are downright sneaky about the approach they use to engage us in these issues. They entice us into the worlds of culture and language by inviting us to reflect on our own cultural and linguistic experiences, resources, and idiosyncrasies on the way to understanding and appreciating the resources that linguistically diverse students—immigrant or otherwise—

will bring to their classrooms. They accomplish this gentle persuasion by sharing many examples from their own experiences—some from their personal experiences as students, others from their experience as teachers, and still others are based on stories that their students and student teachers have related to them. But it is these stories that really ground the book. They animate the abstract principles on which the book is based, giving life to ideas such as cultural relevance and the unintended consequences of linguistic ignorance.

A word about the pedagogical underpinnings of the book. There is an interesting tension in the pedagogy advocated for teachers who work with English learners. There is a strong commitment to constructivist principles of teaching, in which pedagogy begins and ends with the resources that students bring to the learning environment. Unearthing and then using what students know and can do as the basis for teaching anything new is a consistent theme in the book. But that commitment is balanced by an advocacy of explicit teaching, especially when it comes to key language and literacy skills and important knowledge of content and language. This is a healthy tension—one that insures that students will always be learning what's new in relation to what they already know (that always reduces the learning burden) just as surely as it guarantees that teachers will provide all the scaffolding necessary for students to outgrow themselves as learners.

A final comment about the book. It is not the kind of book that students are likely to sell back to campus bookstore at the end of the semester. Instead current and future teachers will keep it and make it a part of their professional libraries—returning to it again and again as they encounter the new students who bring yet a new set of learning challenges—and resources—to the classroom. Both the book and the ideas in it will wear well.

P. David Pearson
Berkeley, California
December 2012

ACKNOWLEDGMENTS

I am thankful to my colleagues from Commonwealth Campuses at Penn State who participated in English Language Learning Disciplinary Community retreats. They traveled many miles to State College, Pennsylvania each summer between 2009 and 2012 to share their wisdom about preparing future teachers to teach English language learners. My students in CI280 have inspired me to become a better teacher every day with their passion for teaching and commitment for improving the lives of others. I am grateful to them all.

I am indebted to numerous teachers. Three most important teachers are P. David Pearson, Meredith McLellan, and my first grade teacher who warmed my hand in her coat pocket while walking me home. I am also indebted to teachers from Spartan Village and Red Cedar Elementary Schools in East Lansing, Michigan. These two schools served as an intellectual reservoir for many emerging teacher education scholars until they closed their doors. Teachers from Eakin Elementary School, especially Beth Asbell, in Nashville, Tennessee, have a special place in my heart because of their knowledge and passion for teaching.

My co-author, Pat Hinchey, has been a saint. Without her gifted writing and editing skills (and her big heart), this book would have never been completed. My family and friends have been an everlasting source of hope, inspiration, and comfort. I am so grateful to Lisa Sensale and Jennifer Danrige-Turner for their friendship. My daughter, Susan Moon, has helped me remember the power of good teachers (as she always talks about why she loves her teachers). My son, Hoh Moon, and my husband, Jong-Yeul Moon, have shown me the courage to get up and continue moving on toward our goals in life.

Lastly, I am indebted to future teachers who want to give their lives to educate future global citizens. It is my earnest hope that this book provides intellectual and practical guidance for these aspiring teachers. This book is dedicated to them.

Youb Kim

Without Youb's initiative and intelligence (and unwavering faith in magic), this book wouldn't exist. Without Chris Myers' unflagging patience with frantic emails...well, let's not go there. Without Vicki Kay

Carter having charged in on her white horse (yet again), this book wouldn't have so few errors (the remaining ones are assuredly mine). Thanks to Youb for the journey, and to Chris and Vicki for helping maintain my sanity as the clock ticked down.

Pat Hinchey

CHAPTER ONE

Imperatives

Why Should You Care?

At a time when this book barely existed in our minds—when not a word of it was actually on paper—we were already wrestling with the Chapter One problem that any author of any book faces: *How do I make readers care about this topic?* We knew that the people most likely to read this book would be teacher education students, and that they would likely be enrolled in a course focused on teaching English Language Learners (ELLs). And, we knew they would probably be in the course not because they particularly wanted to be, but because it was required—perhaps because of state guidelines. In that context, the course might seem one of many to get out of the way, like a math or music elective. And, since few of us like being forced to do anything, we knew our readers might approach this first page with little enthusiasm.

Perhaps we're wrong, and you (yes, you who are reading right now) may wonder why we presume to be able to read your mind. Perhaps you feel differently: perhaps you look forward to working in a multicultural classroom and are eager to learn about how to work productively with children whose first language isn't English. We hope so, and we would be glad to be wrong. But: we've been teaching a state-mandated course to some pretty typical college students—and they've not been shy about telling us their thoughts as our course began.

> *Kids who can't speak English? They don't belong in U.S. schools to begin with. Why should we have to cater to them?*

Oh. Well. That's not a great starting point. But let's start there anyway, because we know that's where many (though certainly not all) teacher education students are as they begin preparing to work with ELLs.

We will have several things to say later about whether children who don't speak English "belong" in U.S. schools and about whether learning to teach them effectively is the same thing as "catering" to them. We suspect, however, that the best answer to the question of *Why should we have to learn this?* comes not from us, but instead from others with first-hand experience in classrooms. We'll begin, then, with voices from the classroom that may provide the best insight into why so many educators and politicians believe that better preparation for teachers is critical—and even overdue.

Behind the Acronym: Voices from the Classroom

ELLs and their friends have offered many snapshots of classroom life that offer insight into the kinds of experiences ELLs frequently have in schools:

> *One young Muslim reported that his homeroom teacher would often duck when he entered the classroom, saying, "You don't have a bomb in that backpack, do you?" The rest of the class had a good laugh, and this student felt compelled to laugh along throughout the school year.*[1]

> *One teacher I had distrusted Asians—she said that Asians would all study together and cheat. My sister—who was in the same class with this teacher—and I talked about it, and we really emphasized our Americanness or our "whiteness" so that this teacher wouldn't associate us with the stereotype that she had.*

> *My name [Dhayal] is supposed to be pronounced Dah-YAHL, but it wasn't easy to pronounce for most people. I remember around 2nd grade, some people started making fun and I started crying. It made me feel kind of inferior to the others. So when I came to high school I just told everybody to pronounce my name Dial. It's a lot easier to say, so that's what most people call me now.*

> *What bothers me a lot is ignorance—people not realizing the difference between someone who's Japanese, someone who's Chinese, someone who's Korean, and just tending to classify them as one big word—Asian—when you wouldn't classify an Italian and a Polish person as the same thing.*

> *One of my Korean friends feels like people exclude him. But of course they do exclude him: He can't communicate as well, he dresses differ-*

ent, he's outcast. And so you end up with a lot of little Asian cliques that speak their same language, and their English hasn't advanced, and people identify them as FOB—"Fresh Off the Boat."[2]

Some comments made by Euro-American students to or about new-comer students included: "Don't speak Spanish here, go back to Mexico;" "All Hispanics are knife-carriers;" "Why don't you ride your camel [said by a white student to an Arabic-speaking student] back to your country!;" and "They [newcomer students] don't belong here, we [Euro-Americans] made this country."(p. 2)[3]

I'd get so tired, my head would hurt. All day, I sit in classes and hear English, English, English, and try so hard to understand, but I do not understand. I was afraid the teacher would call on me. I was trying to hear a word I knew. I was trying to figure out my science and my math. In the morning time it was better. I'd think, today I will understand. But by lunch my head was hurting, and I felt despair. By the last class in the day, I couldn't even listen any more—it was so hard. I just sat there and nothing made sense. (p. 93)[4]

I remember all the classmates make fun of me because I couldn't spoke English. I felt very upset because I didn't have no friends who can help me with my work, and it was very hard for me to understand the teacher. The teacher didn't see me. I felt I wasn't there at all. (p. 96)

How can we learn English if no one speak it with us? No Americans speak with us. A friend would be best, but it is a puzzle. If you don't speak English you can't have American friend. So how do we learn English? (p. 98)

These are discouragingly typical experiences for newcomer students—who aren't responsible for the family's immigration decisions, who arrive anxious about what will happen in an entirely new environment, and who are often inexpressibly sad to leave a familiar home, good friends and loving relatives behind.

Consider the price of coming to the United States for these young people. Invisibility—or worse, as they are prejudged as cheats or teased as would-be terrorists. Loss of identity, as they are no longer recognized as Vietnamese or Colombian and indiscriminately categorized as *Asian* or *Latino*—as they lose even their names when Americans invent new ones for them. Open ridicule, as in nicknames like FOB, *Fresh Off the Boat.* Loneliness, as others ignore them—depriving them of friendship and any help friends might offer with learning English or navigating American culture. Frustration and despair as they try and try to understand but find the language an impermeable barrier.

It's difficult to believe that anyone preparing to teach would want to inflict such pain on *any* student, because people who want to teach generally are sincerely interested in students' well-being. However, when teachers don't know how to work with these students, or when they confuse teasing with painful stereotyping, then even the best-intentioned teachers can unintentionally deny ELLs a positive and productive educational experience. The first and most compelling reason to learn about working with ELLs, then, is that many of them suffer terribly every day when others know nothing about them and have no desire to learn.

ELLs are children and adolescents like those found anywhere, and they want the same things other young people do: classmates who will laugh with them rather than at them, who will help them rather than hurt them, and teachers with a little patience who understand they *want* to learn and are trying as hard as they can to learn. What student doesn't want exactly the same things?

Tomorrow's teachers typically imagine themselves having a strong, positive impact on their students by inspiring them to have big dreams, or getting them excited about a particular subject, or simply being at least one adult who genuinely *cares* about them. Newcomer students desperately need their teachers to have dreams for *them* as well, to genuinely care about *them* as well. Newcomer students deserve good treatment for the same reasons as poor students, rich students, black students, white students and students with special needs: they are human beings with feelings, and many of them will be tomorrow's workers and parents and neighbors.

It helps no one for any child or adolescent to feel embarrassed, unwanted, inferior, invisible, or just plain stupid. Teachers have a responsibility to teach *every* student in their classrooms—*every* student—not just those who look and sound like the teacher. While we don't think teachers intend to be mean or to shortchange students whose first language is not English, we do think the kinds of painful and frustrating experiences reported above often continue because teachers know little about who these students are and haven't had the training they need to build bridges and to support newcomers' learning. States have begun mandating the kind of teacher education this text provides precisely in order to address those problems.

Beyond the Acronym: Schools Failing Students

From our perspective, making the school experience painful for children and adolescents because they don't speak English is a critical ethical issue and reason enough to require more from teacher education programs. But, in recent years, there has also been a compelling practical reason: the *No Child Left Behind Act* (NCLB) of 2001 mandated that schools make sure that all student subgroups—including ELLs—meet specified academic standards. It also mandated extensive standardized testing as a way to monitor school performance. Schools that failed to serve ELLs or any other subgroup effectively over time faced increasingly severe penalties, including mass firings of teachers or school closings. As we wrote this text, NCLB had not been reauthorized and its fate remained uncertain—especially since the Obama administration had issued so many waivers to so many states that observers wondered whether the legislation had been nullified for all practical purposes.[5] However, the Obama administration has vigorously promoted the use of students' standardized test scores to evaluate the performance of teachers (as will be discussed in more detail later), so whatever the fate of the actual legislation, the relentless testing NCLB brought to American schools is unlikely to fade anytime soon.

While NCLB has been controversial for several reasons, many people believe that the scrutiny it has brought to the performance of particular groups of students has turned a much needed spotlight on troubled areas of American education. Results for ELLs have been largely dismal both before and after the law's implementation, and many schools have been found failing and forced to reconsider their efforts and programs. One 2004 research report that analyzed state test data, for example, found ELLs' school performance to be as much as 20 to 30 percentage points lower than that of other students, with little improvement even over several years.[6] A 2010 report indicated that, while there have been some gains in recent years, large gaps remain and are a national concern:

- **Very large differences in percentages proficient exist between English language learners and other students.** Of the 35 states with sufficient data in high school reading, 27 states had differences in the percentage proficient of more than 30 percentage points between ELLs and students who are not English language learners, and 18 states had differences of more than 40 percentage points.

- **Percentages proficient for English language learners vary widely by state, more so than for students who are not ELLs.** In one state, for example, 87% of high school ELLs scored proficient in reading, while in another just 6% of ELLs reached proficiency, a staggering disparity between states. The comparable range for non-ELLs was a high of 94% and a low of 38%. Even after considering the differences that exist among states in standards, assessments, testing policies, and demographics, the low performance of ELLs in some states is surely a cause for concern.[7]

Such disparities are untenable in a country with a core commitment to equal opportunity. In addition, they can exacerbate an existing unemployment problem: students who continuously fail often drop out without earning the minimal work credential of a high school diploma.

Poor academic performance is a particular problem for Latinos. While on the whole they made progress on state tests between 2002 and 2008, large gaps in achievement remain, with many Latino students not reaching the levels they would need to succeed either in college or a career. They performed well below Asian and white students on NCLB-mandated math and reading tests at grades 4 and 8, as well as at the high school level.[8] Most alarmingly, some 41% of Latinos leave high school without a diploma—a much higher rate than Whites (14%) or Asians (15%).[9]

Nor are Latinos the only group of ELLs known to be having difficulty. Although a segment of Asian students excel in school—giving rise to the stereotype of the Asian "whiz kid"—not all fare so well. In some states, subgroups of Asian students lag far behind their white peers in certain subjects and grades.[10] Explanations for the discrepancy highlight the fact that the Asian subgroup includes large numbers of recent immigrants or refugees who do not know English.

The known gaps in achievement for ELLs and the increasing number of ELLs in public school classrooms are the primary reasons that policymakers have been working toward better teacher preparation. Teachers with skills for effective performance in multicultural classrooms are both very much needed and very much wanted.

Moving beyond the Myths: Facts and Figures

Thanks to a great deal of nearly hysterical political posturing on the issue of immigration, many Americans believe that *English Language Learner* really means *Mexican*, and *Mexican* means undocumented, poor adults with no skills flooding into the United States to take advantage of public benefits. This nearly cartoonish oversimplification obscures a far more complex reality:

- The majority of Spanish-speaking immigrants are Mexicans, but the Spanish-speaking immigrant population also includes Cubans, Colombians, Dominicans, Puerto Ricans (who are U.S. citizens), Salvadorans and others from Central and South America. While they may share one language, these nationalities have distinct histories and cultures.

- In 2010, of the 50+ million immigrants from Spanish-speaking countries in the U.S., only about one in five (some 11+ million) were in the country illegally.[11] The vast majority (some 80%) of the Spanish-speaking population in the United States resides there legally.

- Many immigrant adults, Spanish-speakers and others, did flee extreme poverty in their homelands—but many immigrant adults are also successful and skilled workers and professionals, and they may have fled war or persecution rather than poverty.

Moreover, immigration patterns may be changing. Although Mexicans have certainly comprised the largest segment of the immigrant population in the United States for some time, Asian immigrants outnumbered them in 2010. The Asian group includes Chinese, Filipino, Indian, Vietnamese, Koreans, Japanese and others—with each also having distinct histories and cultures.[12]

Also in contrast to the dominant Mexican stereotype, one in four newcomer students speaks a language other than Spanish. A 2002 report found the next most widely spoken languages among public school students to be Vietnamese, Hmong, Chinese, Cantonese, and Korean; another 450 newcomer languages include Arabic, Armenian, Chuukese, French, Haitian Creole, Hindi, Japanese, Khmer, Lao, Mandarin, Marshallese, Navajo, Polish, Portuguese, Punjabi, Russian, Serbo-Croatian, Tagalog, and Urdu.[13]

Moreover, children who don't speak English may have parents who do. Highly skilled professionals from other countries often work in the U.S. either temporarily or permanently. Even though they learned English at some point, their children may not have had the same opportunity. In addition, many Americans adopt children from foreign countries.

How many students are we talking about overall? Over 5 million—an increase of 57% in ten years, with the number continuing to rise. Stated more practically: about one in every nine students is an English language learner.[14] As to whether or not these students "belong" in American schools: 79% of them were born in the United States and are U.S. citizens.[15] As the sheer numbers of ELLS has been rising, there has been a correlative rise in the percentage of teachers with at least one ELL in their classroom: 60%.[16] Teacher education students who grew up in predominantly white areas and went to virtually all-white schools may imagine teaching only white, English-speaking students.[17] However, the reality is that anyone who expects to staff a classroom in the future should expect to routinely find ELLs among their students, since that is already the case for nearly two out of three teachers. Yet despite the fact that the ELL population has been steadily increasing, there is a gap in teacher preparation. In 2006 a survey of over 1,200 teachers, 57% reported that they didn't know enough to work effectively with ELLs.[18]

Given how frequently media reports incorrectly suggest that most ELLs come from undocumented Mexican families, several points from this brief overview are worth reiterating and remembering. First, the vast majority of newcomer children whose first language is not English are in the U.S. *legally*, and they are *legally* entitled to a public education. Second, it is smart policy to educate ELLs no matter their immigration status, since many are likely to remain in the country throughout their adult lives; a good education will prepare them to be productive workers, good citizens and supportive neighbors. Third, ELLs are not an undifferentiated mass, but instead millions of unique individuals. There is no single way to say who "they" are, because they are both rich and poor;

they may—or may not—have been born in another country; they speak well over 400 different languages; and, they come from staggeringly diverse cultures. Moreover, tomorrow's teachers can expect to have at least one ELL in their classrooms, and likely more as the years go by. Meanwhile, today's teachers are indicating that they are largely unprepared to work productively with ELLs, and they need and want to know more about how to work with them.

Professionalism

We have still not exhausted our answers to the question of why future teachers should take this book and other lessons in working with ELLs seriously. Yet another reason is that as professionals, teachers have an ethical responsibility to their students—just as doctors have an ethical responsibility to their patients. No doctor would stand in an emergency room and say "I don't understand the language this patient is speaking, so there's nothing I can do to help." Nor should teachers take that stance in relation to any student. Several professional organizations as well as several government bodies have made clear that as professionals, teachers must work as hard for ELLs as they do for others.

Unions and Professionalism

Although many people think of teachers unions as organizations interested only in contract negotiations, the reality is that they are professional organizations that help members understand issues in education and that publicize expectations for professional performance. Both of the two major teachers unions in the U.S.—the National Education Association (NEA) and the American Federation of Teachers (AFT)—have taken public positions that make clear their expectations for teachers of ELLs.

National Education Association. The NEA's Code of Ethics, which defines expectations for teacher professionalism, indicates that teachers are bound "to help each student realize his or her potential as a worthy and effective member of society."[19] The Code specifically prohibits teachers from discriminating on the basis of nationality; teachers are not to exclude any students from activities, deny them benefits, or privilege some over others. Obviously, a teacher who has no idea how to work with English language learners will deny them the benefits of effective classroom instruction and, intentionally or not, shut them out of most classroom activities.

Recognizing that many teachers have not received the training they need to provide effective instruction to ELLs and that the current achievement gap must be closed, the NEA has taken several steps to promote better, more effective classroom conditions. These include efforts to ensure better preparation for classroom teachers because "General education teachers need practical, research-based information, resources, and strategies to teach, evaluate, and nurture ELL students."[20] There is so much to know, and so many variables in dealing with specific ELL populations, that the union also strongly supports "professional development opportunities for general education teachers at every stage in their careers [as] a key step toward ensuring great teachers in great public schools for all students."[21]

American Federation of Teachers. Like the NEA, the AFT has called on a variety of stakeholders to improve the education of ELLs. In its 2006 position paper titled *Where We Stand: English Language Learners*, the union argues that much more teacher preparation is needed for several reasons, including that: teacher education programs typically have not provided ELL coursework or relevant in-school experience; there is a nationwide shortage of teachers and other staff prepared to work with ELLs; and often, unsupervised paraprofessionals rather than teachers provide instruction to ELLs.[22] Also like the NEA, the AFT urges a variety of stakeholders, including the federal government, to take a variety of steps to improve current conditions. For schools of education, AFT recommends that all teacher education programs include both coursework and experiences that can help prepare teachers to meet ELLs' instructional needs.

Standards and Professionalism

Because professionals affect the well-being of their clients, it's important that their competence be documented before and during their professional practice. Various processes are used for such documentation. Doctors, for example, must pass rigorous exams before states license them, and hospitals monitor patient outcomes to be sure a particular doctor isn't routinely failing to treat patients appropriately. In the case of teachers, one documentation process known as *accreditation* involves an out-side agency determining whether teacher education programs not only provide their students with professional knowledge and skills, but also nurture appropriate attitudes, commonly known as *dispositions*. Teacher education programs are also expected to document their graduates' competence, and there are a variety of procedures routinely used to evaluate teachers' performance in the classroom, as discussed in more detail below.

Before it's possible to assess either programs or performance, how-ever, it's necessary to define *which* knowledge, skills and attitudes are those a teacher must have. Teacher educators must know what evalua-tors of their programs expect students to learn, and teachers must know what evaluators of their classroom performance will be looking for. Spe-cific expectations for teacher performance are called *standards*, and various organizations have developed various standards for teacher preparation and performance.

Standards for Teacher Preparation. As this book was being written, two major organizations that accredit teacher education programs were merging. The National Council for Accreditation of Teacher Education (NCATE) and the Teacher Education Alliance Council (TEAC) have come together to form a new organization known as the Council for the Ac-creditation of Educator Preparation (CAEP). CAEP has drafted one new set of standards based on commonalities in NCATE and TEAC's earlier standards. We can expect the new CAEP standards to be those guiding future accreditation for many teacher education programs.

In terms of teacher knowledge, skills and dispositions, one CAEP standard indicates that teacher education programs will prepare stu-dents to "nurture the academic and social development of all students through professional dispositions such as caring, fairness, and the belief that all students can learn."[23] The expectation that teachers will be committed to teaching *all* students in their care, and not just some of them, echoes the ethical responsibility detailed in the NEA Code of Con-duct. While the CAEP document refers specifically only to "all students," because the earlier NCATE standards mentioned ELLs and the TEAC standards mentioned "multicultural" populations, there is no doubt that teacher education programs are expected to prepare their students to work effectively with ELLs and all other subgroups.

In addition to CAEP, states also assess teacher education programs, using their own state standards as a basis for state accreditation. Increasingly, states are imposing specific requirements for preparation to work with ELLs. A 2008 study from the National Clearinghouse for English Language Acquisition reported that four states (Arizona, California, Florida and New York) had such requirements and, as expected at that time, Pennsylvania became the fifth state to do so.[24] (Indeed, this book has grown out of Pennsylvania's detailed requirement for teacher preparation.) Some 17 states, however, mentioned ELLs in their standards for certification without mandating how exactly programs and candidates would develop or exhibit expertise specific to the ELL population. Only 15 states at the time of the report had no requirement that all teachers be prepared to work specifically with ELLs. Given the continued gap in ELL performance and union efforts to promote awareness of the need to educate general classroom teachers to work with ELLs, it is likely that state requirements will steadily increase.

Standards for Student Performance. As noted above, the *No Child Left Behind* (NCLB) has imposed strict requirements that include monitoring the academic performance of ELLs. As we have also explained, assessing something requires first being clear about expectations. To make sure that teachers know exactly what their students are expected to know and be able to do, states have academic standards for several subjects and in several grades. For example, students in first grade might be expected to capitalize the pronoun *I*, those in third grade to know how to use *its* and *it's* correctly in their writing, and high school seniors to avoid run-on sentences or fragments in multi-paragraph essays. Standardized tests at those levels would check to be sure those skills were in place.

For many reasons, there has been a nationwide movement away from earlier individual state standards and instead toward a single set of national standards (Common Core Standards), which have now been adopted by 45 states and three U. S. territories.[25] Because many politicians are aware that too few ELLs are mastering academic content as expected, there has been an ambitious effort to clarify how teachers can work toward national standards with ELLs and monitor progress of ELLs in their classrooms.

A consortium of states known as WIDA (World-Class Instructional Design and Assessment) has sponsored the creation of standards for

English Language Proficiency, which offer extensive support to class-room teachers. These standards not only define levels of English language proficiency (ELP), but they span all grade levels and several specific subject areas. For example, a third grade teacher might consult the standards to determine how proficient a new student is in English, while a ninth grade social studies teacher might consult them to see how an ELL at a particular level might be expected to convey understanding of a unit on forms of government—by labeling or drawing pictures, for example. In short, these standards provide detailed information about how teachers can engage ELLs at various levels with academic subject matter as well how they can monitor students' progress both in content and in English language growth.

With so many standards in place to shape not only teacher preparation but teacher performance, teacher educators and teachers are both expected to have a clear and detailed picture of their responsibilities in terms of student learning. Just as standards for teacher preparation are the basis for evaluation of preparation programs, the standards for what students should know and be able to do provide the basis for evaluating student learning. National standards in various subject areas allow for national tests of students—and the implications for teacher assessment are enormous.

Implications for Assessment of Tomorrow's Teachers

While the long-term fate of NCLB is undecided, it is unlikely that the widespread standardized testing it mandated will disappear for at least two reasons. First, many states used various forms of standardized testing even before NCLB was implemented, and second, the emphasis on examining the performance of specific subgroups of students has helped schools identify areas where they needed to target improvements. Standardized tests, then, are likely to remain a fact of life for tomorrow's teachers—as is their recently developed use as a measure of teacher effectiveness. With test data readily available, many people with much influence (including politicians as well as philanthropists) have argued that student test scores should be used as a measure of teacher effectiveness.

On the surface, there appears to be some sense to this idea: shouldn't we be able to expect that if a teacher is doing a good job, students will demonstrate significant growth over a school year? Certainly, a class-room where no student seems to learn anything suggests there may well be a problem with teacher effectiveness. However: critics note that there are many factors affecting students' performance that are out of teachers' control, including such things as whether the school can afford basic supplies like books and pencils, whether sick children have access to medical care and medications, and whether they have enough to eat or even a place to sleep at night. Few people deny that such factors affect what teachers can accomplish, and yet despite that obvious complication, student test scores are increasingly being used to evaluate teachers.

The evaluation of teachers based on student test scores uses a proc-ess known as *value-added assessment*, or VAA. Several statisticians have devised formulas that they believe can allow for such factors as poverty and the effectiveness of earlier teachers and can predict accurately how much growth a student might be expected to show in a year. These pre-dictions are then used to assess classroom teachers: the teacher's effec-tiveness depends upon whether student growth meets, exceeds or falls short of the predicted level. Although there has been extensive criticism of VAA as misleading and wildly inaccurate in many cases (in a mountain of research that lies beyond the scope of this text), and although differ-ent formulas produce distinctly different evaluations of the same teacher, politicians and policymakers have successfully promoted the widespread use of VAA for teacher assessment.

A 2007 study by Florida State University found 15 states using forms of VAA, but at that time only four had mandated its use.[26] In 2009, how-ever, the Obama administration launched its Race to the Top (RTT) grant program, which required participating states to mandate student test scores as one measure of teacher effectiveness. Eleven states[27] and the District of Columbia successfully competed for RTT grants in 2010, and seven states did so in 2011[28]—so that as this book was being writ-ten, at least 18 states as well as the District of Columbia had mandated VAA as a measure of teacher effectiveness.

Tomorrow's teachers can expect that their performance will be as-sessed at least partially on their students' standardized test scores, in-cluding those of their ELL students. In such an environment, it is a measure of self-defense for students to prepare themselves as well as possible to meet the classroom challenges lying ahead.

A More Positive Perspective

We began this chapter with a negative: the negative attitude many students exhibit at the beginning of a course in strategies for working with ELLs. At this point, we hope that we have helped readers abandon common but inaccurate ideas about ELLs and persuaded them that there are ethical as well as practical reasons for learning strategies for working productively with this population. We also hope, however, that our discussion here has not made working with ELLs sound like a heavy burden. It is a heavy responsibility, to be sure, but not a burden. Instead, it is a privilege and pleasure to have ELLs in the classroom because they bring a richness of experience with them. If ELLs are actively welcomed into a classroom community and asked to share their experiences and thoughts, they can give their teachers and classmates a window into far distant parts of the world. ELLs may have much to learn, but they also have much to teach—as we'll discuss in the pages ahead.

Explorations

1. Only a small percentage of students whose first language is Spanish are in the United States illegally, but inaccurate ideas about their experience helps promote discrimination against any Spanish-speaking student. To develop an informed understanding of some undocumented students' experiences, watch the video *Wetback: The Undocumented Documentary* (2005), which makes clear the incredible sacrifices that desperate people from Central America and Mexico make to enter the United States. Be aware that it is extremely painful to watch—and it will be impossible to forget.

2. Many people with no experience with English language learners find it difficult to imagine that they can succeed in school, especially if they are poor. For a firsthand look at an incredibly diverse school where students have come from not only poor but war-torn countries, watch the video *A Family of Many Nations* (2003). This video offers a portrait of a school where students come from fifty different countries and speak twenty-seven different languages. The difference a caring and skilled staff can make to the future of these children and others like them is nothing short of amazing.

3. Research demographics of your state and nearby states to determine whether and to what extent the populations may be changing. How many English language learners attend schools in those states? How much change have the states experienced in recent years?

4. Research requirements for teacher preparation and teacher assessment in your state and nearby states. Are tomorrow's teachers expected to be prepared to work with ELLs? Do any of the states require that student test scores be part of teacher evaluations?

5. One thing that a professional needs is an inquiring mind—the kind of mind that moves people to poke around resources for no particular purpose, just to see what might be interesting. To begin developing this disposition, visit the *Teaching Tolerance* website at http://www.tolerance.org. Type into the search box: English language learners. Browse the articles that come up, and prepare to discuss what you found interesting with your classmates.

Notes

1   Joshi, K. Y. (2007, Fall). 'Because I had a turban.' *Teaching Tolerance, 32*. Retrieved from http://www.tolerance.org/magazine/number-32-fall-2007/because-i-had-turban

2   *Teaching Tolerance, 10*. (1996, Fall). In our own words. Retrieved from http://www.tolerance.org/magazine/number-10-fall-1996/our-own-words

3   Brantmeier, E. (2012). Wounded in the field: Peacebuilding at Junction High School. Unpublished manuscript.

4   Olsen, L. (1997). *Made in America*. New York: The New Press.

5   Rich, M. (2012, July 6). 'No Child' law whittled down by White House. *The New York Times*. Retrieved from http://www.nytimes.com/2012/07/06/education/no-child-left-behind-whittled-down-under-obama.html?pagewanted=all

6   Abedi, J., & Dietel, R. (2004, Winter, Policy Brief 7). Challenges in the No Child Left Behind Act for English Language Learners. Retrieved from http://www.cse.ucla.edu/products/policy/cresst_policy7.pdf

7   Chudowsky, N., & Chudowsky, V. (2010, April 7). Has progress been made in raising achievement for English Language Learners? Retrieved from http://www.cep-dc.org/displayDocument.cfm?DocumentID=323

8   Kober, N., Chudowsky, N., Chudowsky, C., & Dietz, S. (2010, June 30). Improving achievement for the growing Latino population is critical to the nation's future. Retrieved from http://www.cep-dc.org/displayDocument.cfm?DocumentID=133

9   Fry, R. (2010, May 13). Hispanics, high school dropouts and the GED. Retrieved from *www.pewhispanic.org/files/reports/122.pdf*

10   Kober, N., Chudowsky, N., Chudowsky, V., & Dietz, S. (2010, June 30). Policy implica-
     tions of trends for Asian American students. Retrieved from http://www.cep-
     dc.org/displayDocument.cfm?DocumentID=142

11   Pew Hispanic Center. (n.d.) Latinos' lives by the numbers. Retrieved June 18, 2012,
     from http://www.pewhispanic.org/

12   El Nasser, H. (2012, June 19). Study: Asian Americans value hard work, family. *USA
     Today*. Retrieved from http://www.usatoday.com/news/nation/story/2012-06-
     18/asian-american-study/55677050/1

13   Kindler, A.L. (2002, October). Survey of the states' Limited English Proficient Students
     and available educational programs and services 2000–2001 summary report. Retrieved
     from http://www.ncela.gwu.edu/files/rcd/BE021853/Survey_of_the_States.pdf

14   Wetzel, J. (2012, March 15). Educational trajectories of English Language Learners
     examined. Retrieved July 1, 2012, from http://news.vanderbilt.edu/2012/03/ edu-
     cational-trajectories-of-ell/

15   García, E. E., Jensen, B. T., & Scribner, K. P. (2009, April). The demographic impera-
     tive. *Educational Leadership, 66 (7)*. Retrieved from http://12.4.125.3/ASCD/pdf/
     journals/ed_lead/el200904_garcia.pdf

16   American Federation of Teachers. (AFT). (2006,November). Where we stand: Eng-
     lish language learners. *AFT Convention Resolution*. Retrieved from http://www.aft.
     org/pdfs/teachers/wwsell1106.pdf

17   National Center for Education Information (NCEI). (2005, August 18). News release:
     Profile of teachers in the U.S. 2005. Retrieved from http://www.ncei.com/
     POT05PRESSREL3.htm

18   National Education Association. (2011). Professional development for general edu-
     cation teachers of ELLs. *NEA Policy Brief.* Retrieved from http://www.nea.org/ as-
     sets/docs/PB32_ELL11.pdf

19   National Education Association. (1975[adopted]) Code of ethics. Retrieved from
     http://www.nea.org/home/30442.htm

20   National Education Association. (2011). Professional development for general edu-
     cation teachers of ELLs. *NEA Policy Brief.* Retrieved from http://www.nea.org/ as-
     sets/docs/PB32_ELL11.pdf

21   National Education Association. (2011). Professional development for general edu-
     cation teachers of ELLs. *NEA Policy Brief.* Retrieved from http://www.nea.org/ as-
     sets/docs/PB32_ELL11.pdf

22   American Federation of Teachers. (AFT). (2006, November). Where we stand: Eng-
     lish language learners. *AFT Convention Resolution.* Retrieved from http://www.
     aft.org/pdfs/teachers/wwsell1106.pdf

23   NCATE/TEAC Design Team. (2010, October 15). Report and Recommendation of the
     NCATE/TEAC Design Team to Our Respective Boards of Directors. Retrieved from
     http://www.teac.org/wp-content/uploads/2010/10/Design-Team-Report1.pdf

24   National Clearinghouse for English Language Acquisition (NCELA). (2008). State
     requirements for pre-service teachers of ELLs. *Educating English Language Learn-*

ers: Building capacity. Roundtable Report, Volume III. Retrieved from http://www.ncela.gwu.edu/files/uploads/3/EducatingELLsBuildingTeacherCapacityVol3.pdf

25 Common Core State Standards Initiative. (2012). In the states. Retrieved from http://www.corestandards.org/in-the-states

26 Shurtleff, D.S., & Loredo, J. (2008). Beyond No Child Left Behind: Value-added assessment of student progress. Retrieved from http://www.ncpa.org/pub/ba636/

27 Delaware, Florida, Georgia, Hawaii, Maryland, Massachusetts, New York, North Carolina, Ohio, Rhode Island, and Tennessee

28 Arizona, Colorado, Illinois, Kentucky, Louisiana, Pennsylvania, and New Jersey

CHAPTER TWO

Culture

Beyond Tacos and Lo Mein

In the university classes we teach, we routinely ask students to describe their culture. Since our students (who are probably similar to most students reading this text) come primarily from families who have lived in the United States for three or more generations, their first reaction is often a protest: "But I don't *have* any particular culture. I'm American. I'm just normal," they tell us.

Just normal. But what does that mean?

Ironically, when students use the word *normal* to describe themselves, they are actually identifying themselves as members of a culture in which they are so completely immersed that they literally don't see or recognize it. A common metaphor for the situation is that of a fish in the sea, which cannot recognize *the sea* in the same way as someone standing on the shore would. In addition to indicating they are members of some culture they call *normal*, the students are also indicating they are *not* members of some other cultures—which, since they are not members, they are implying are somehow *not-normal*. That is, even as students deny having a culture, their response indicates they do have a sense of "I am a member of *this* group but not *those others*." Indeed, asked to describe what *normal* means, they often say "Well, I mean, I'm not African American or Mexican or anything like that." They may be unaware of doing it, but our students routinely sort people into groups, with people who resemble them being considered *normal*, and others unlike them in various ways (having different skin colors, for example, or wearing dashikis or thobes) falling into the unspoken category of *not-normal*.

Does this perspective mean students who consider themselves *normal* actually have some kind of conscious or unconscious superiority complex? Well: yes and no. Yes, because being *normal* seems more desirable than being *not normal,* or *abnormal*. Who wants to be described as *abnormal*? But at the same time: no, those students are not particularly arrogant or conceited people. Instead, they are simply human, and they are behaving as all humans everywhere and always behave: they form groups, and members of each group typically consider all other groups inferior in some way. For a simple demonstration, think back to high school. It's a safe bet that various groups within the student body included nerds and jocks, and that those groups (and others) probably had a lot of nasty things to say about each other.

Consider the implications of this routine normal/not-normal distinction for classrooms, where children from a wide variety of homes come together to learn daily: Are all students likely to learn equally well—or even to receive equal attention and support from the teacher—when there is an unspoken assumption that some of them are *normal* (however that may be defined at a particular place and time) and some are *not normal*? To be honest—humans being as they are—it's highly unlikely. Most people, including children, are uncomfortable in groups where they are aware of being *different*, so they often focus on trying to say and do the right things to fit in. Both their discomfort and their focus on fitting in are distractions, making learning more difficult. Moreover, most people are routinely more attentive and generous to others who seem *the same*. Teachers, being people, have the same tendencies and are often more patient with students who aren't different, who don't have special needs, than they are with those who fall into the *not normal* category. It's important to remember that these generalizations are not intended to be criticisms of teachers or anyone else. Instead, as we'll discuss in more detail below, they are simply descriptions of what researchers and scholars know about human behavior.

While the normal/not normal dichotomy may itself be *normal* in that everyone makes such distinctions, it cannot be allowed to stand in schools if we are to have truly equitable and nurturing classrooms. No child should be consciously or unconsciously mentally herded into the category of *not normal*, either by classmates or by teachers themselves. The goal of this chapter, therefore, is to help future and practicing teachers deepen their understanding of cultural complexities so that they are prepared to establish classroom norms that will allow *every* child to feel at home. As we'll demonstrate below, insensitivity to cultural issues in the classroom not only interferes with learning, but it also causes many children, including English language learners, substantial pain.

Culture/s: Everyone Has—Many

Wherever there are humans, there is culture, which is perhaps most simply described as patterns of thinking, values and behaviors. We often think of culture in terms of nationality. For example, people living in the United States are generally called Americans, and they typically share some basic beliefs and values. These include the ideas that democracy is the best form of government, that personal freedom is a human right, that competition is a good way to develop personal initiative, and that accumulating more and more money and things is, or should be, everyone's priority. When we take such national norms for granted and assume they provide guidelines for the one best way to live, we are being what is called *ethnocentric*.

Of course, not every American fits the above pattern. Some think, for example, that Americans are too competitive and too fixated on wealth. Such contrary ideas frequently arise because people are never perfect duplicates of each other. For that reason, every culture also contains a number of *subcultures*: smaller groups within the whole with their own characteristic beliefs and values.

For example, people living on the East Coast of the United States are frequently contrasted with people living on the West Coast. Life in New York City is generally considered fast-paced, perhaps even driven, and highly stressful, with workers having little time or attention to devote to personal or family well-being. In contrast, life in California is considered low-key, relaxed, much slower than in the East, with everyone eating only healthful foods and staying physically fit. Of course, the smaller subcultures will always have exceptions within them as well, like the physically fit New Yorker who is content to work 40 hours per week and live modestly, or the obese and wheezing Californian who works 60 hours a week to maintain an extravagant oceanfront home.

Note, too, that in even this simple example, various individual people would "belong" to more than one group—that is, they would be members of various subcultures. On the one hand, they're all Americans; on the other, some Americans are New Yorkers, and some are Californians; some have highly stressful work lives, some have a more relaxed lifestyle; some pursue affluence, others are content with a more modest income; some value physical fitness, others don't mind carrying extra weight.

Geography, or location, is only one of many characteristics that shape cultures and subcultures. Others include gender, as when children are taught that little boys behave *like this* and not *like that*; religion, as when young Christians learn to attend religious rituals on Sundays and young Hindus learn not to eat beef; and values, as when children in authoritarian families learn that obedience is of primary importance, while children in permissive families learn to privilege their own interests and preferences.

As people go about their day, they generally move seamlessly from one subculture to another without noticing. For example, the dutiful daughter may hug her mother goodbye in the morning (as a family member), drive to her high school on the right side of the road (as an American), listen to rock music in the car (as a teen), and stop by the ladies room at school to touch up her makeup before going to class (as a female). In each case, this hypothetical daughter aligns her behavior with what various groups expect: showing affection, driving on the right side of the road, listening to rock, and wearing makeup.

The expected attitudes and behaviors of a particular group constitute the group's *norms*, and those *norms* define what members of each group consider *normal*. Alternatively phrased, *norms* are the patterns or standards against which some things (and people) are measured and judged *normal*, while other things (and people) are measured and judged *not normal*. Precisely because we think of characteristics of our own groups as normal, we rarely recognize them, although we are quick to recognize (and censure) violations of norms. Imagine, for example, how a group of teens in a school parking lot might react to a student arriving blaring opera from the car stereo, or how a group of males in the school's men's room might react to a boy carefully applying tinted lip gloss. Despite rarely being conscious of norms, everyone behaves according to them daily and is quick to notice violations. Even "rebels" tend to be rebellious in the same way, wearing the same kind of clothing, sporting similar hairstyles, and disliking the same *other* groups.

Forming groups and being able to identify who is/isn't in them is simply something that humans do, and have always done. *Why* we humans engage in all this mental sorting and classifying is a topic researchers have been trying to explain for a very long time. It is useful to know a bit about their work before we explore what can and does happen when children who are members of cultures that do not speak English arrive in a classroom of native English speakers.

To Herd Is Human

As the researcher Henri Tafel found as early as 1970, "Socialization into 'groupness' is powerful and unavoidable" (p. 102).[1] Decades of work by social science and humanities researchers have produced a mountain of research that supports Tafel's assertion. As long as there have been people, they have made distinctions and formed groups. That is, they have developed mental categories for *our tribe/other tribes*, or *our country/other countries*, or *our religion/other religions*, or *male/female,* or *our family/other families....* Researchers have also documented two common and important characteristics of groups, each with implications for the classroom. The first is that the characteristics people use to mark off one group from another are often trivial, even meaningless. The second is that typically, each group considers itself superior to other groups, concurrently believing all other groups to be inferior. This assumed superiority of one group over another leads to several problematic results: bias against *others*, unfair distribution of resources, and often even hostility. There are many obvious examples in American history: at various times, Native Americans, Jews, African slaves, and the Irish were all widely considered *less* than human by some White American groups.

Minimal group paradigm is the term scholars use for the finding that people *will* form groups, along with the terms *ingroups* (for the "insiders") and *outgroups* (for the "outsiders"). People will use any available trait to mark off the ingroup from the outgroup, whether the trait has any significance or not. Tafel demonstrated this point convincingly in some well-known experiments. He asked teenage boys to estimate the number of dots projected on a screen and conducted a number of follow-up activities. His findings included that the boys quickly adopted the categories of dot "overestimators" and "underestimators," routinely believed whichever group they were in was superior to the other, and when given the opportunity to portion out rewards, consistently favored their own groups. Results were similar in experiments asking boys to say which of two unfamiliar painters they preferred. The boys did what people do: they developed mental categories based on meaningless traits (ability to guess numbers of dots, liking one painter more than another); they judged their own groups superior; and, they gave members of their own groups preferential treatment when they could.[2]

Although it may be difficult to imagine using such trivial criteria to make value judgments about other people, if we pay attention we can see evidence of just such behavior in daily life. For example, educator Gary Howard (whose work we gratefully acknowledge as an influence on our thinking in this chapter) tells this revealing story:

> In a recent workshop with students from two high schools in the same rural, pre-dominantly White town in upstate New York, the lesson of minimal group distinctions was brought home to me in a rather humorous way. Even though the two schools were virtually indistinguishable demographically, the students from one seemed to invest a great deal of energy in perpetuating a stereotype of students from the other school as a "bunch of hicks." During the workshop this issue of "degrees of hickness" was vigorously debated by students from both schools, with the tension and volume in the room rising as each new attack or counterattack further denigrated members of the opposing group. Determined not to lose the workshop to the heat of such a seemingly insignificant battle, my co-facilitator and I finally called a break and discussed how we might use the "hick" issue as an entrée into our intended discussion of race and gender stereotypes. The perfect teachable moment came when one of the few African American students in the workshop, a young woman who had recently moved to this small town from an urban and highly multicultural neighborhood, said to me, "Mr. Howard, I don't see what all this hassle is about. As far as I'm concerned, they're *all* a bunch of hicks" (1999, pp. 28–29).[3]

Forming groups based on almost any criteria and developing biases against other groups: it's what humans do.

Not surprisingly, researchers have spent much time and effort trying to figure out why this is how people behave, especially in terms of why they exhibit hostility toward other groups. Sometimes the reason is obvious, as when countries go to war over land or power, or when White slave owners rationalized that since Africans were less than human, there could be no moral objection to enslaving them. But even when there is nothing substantial to fight over, human behavior is the same: people stereotype *others*, they exhibit biases against *others*, and they privilege members of their own groups.

If that sounds like a pretty tough characterization, stop for a moment and think about what many Americans first say in reaction to something different: *"That's weird."* The word *weird* isn't a neutral one, like *different.* Weird has the connotations of *abnormal*, or even *bizarre*. It's entirely possible to be biased against something—or someone—from *outside* our own ingroups while being entirely unaware of it because making the ingroup/outgroup distinction so deeply ingrained in human behavior.

Various explanations for bias against outgroups have been offered, including: that people who are frustrated in reaching their own goals vent their frustration through aggression against others who are less powerful (and so less dangerous to attack); that authoritarian personalities motivate some people to despise and dominate other weaker groups; that people find safety and comfort in the familiar and so reject and avoid the unfamiliar; that people vary widely in the value they place on core human values of freedom and equality; and, that people naturally make associations and look for patterns as they learn to make sense of the world, so that stereotyping is a common human activity.[4]

For the purposes of this discussion, we don't need a definitive answer to the question of why people prefer others like themselves and are often antagonistic toward those who are different. In the long run, it doesn't matter whether some people insist on their superiority over other people in order to vent frustration, to feel safe, or to increase their wealth. Instead, it's essential to understand that social scientists have conclusively demonstrated that forming groups and considering members of other groups inferior is typical human behavior.

Since teachers are human, they cannot be immune from this universal human trait. Until they understand that they, too, are members of some specific cultures which function as their ingroup/s, they are unlikely to be aware of their human tendency to privilege children like themselves and to perceive children from outgroups as inherently inferior in some ways. No teacher would mean to discriminate against a child—but to avoid doing so unconsciously, it's necessary to understand the way dominant assumptions about norms play out in classrooms and affect the teaching and learning environment.

Language Norms

Language norms, like other cultural norms, influence the way members of one group interact with members of another. More specifically, language norms in classrooms often generate significant challenges for English language learners in at least two areas—how they are perceived by their teachers and how they see themselves.

Teachers and Language

The characteristics of the ingroups we belong to give us a constellation of traits that provide our identity/ies: "I am *this* and *not that.*" And, once we believe something about ourselves, it becomes extremely difficult to imagine ourselves as something or someone else, especially as members of some outgroup. For example, surely everyone knows at least one person who has said "I'm just not smart" or "I'm just not good at math" or "I'm just not athletic." One of the authors, in fact, said "I'm just not good at math" all the way until her senior year of college—when she encountered a talented math teacher for the first time and learned "I can be darned good at math if I have the right kind of instruction." These ideas about who we are and what we can and can't do have tremendous impact on behavior, as when people rule out career choices because they believe they can't do something well. And as anyone who has attempted to talk another person out of an idea knows, it's tremendously difficult to change self-perceptions. Any experienced teacher can affirm that saying "But you *are* smart" even a thousand times rarely convinces students earning Cs and Ds that they really could do better.

For teachers, perceptions about who can and should learn one or more languages have critical implications both for what they themselves do and for what they expect of students. Few of our teacher education students are fluent in, or even vaguely familiar with, a second language, and many insist "I'm just not good at languages." In other words, in their minds, a bilingual or multilingual person is just not who they are. Their failure to learn a second language may actually be due to poor early instruction (as in the math example above), but no matter the reason for it, the idea that they can't learn a second language is a common one among many Americans, including many who want to be teachers. Only success in learning a second language is likely to change that self-perception, but success is not an option for people who refuse to even attempt a language course because they are convinced they would fail. Thus, it's unlikely that classrooms will soon be fully staffed with bilingual or multilingual teachers, despite the clear need for them indicated by the demographics discussed in Chapter One.

Having a predominantly monolingual teaching force reinforces a classroom definition of *normal* based on language as *people who speak English—and only English.* Even education students familiar with multilingual environments like New York City or San Francisco may, if they have not learned a second language themselves, consider speaking only English the norm. In one sense, this is a reasonable idea: Americans do speak English, and most do speak only English (largely because geography doesn't cause them to interact routinely with speakers of other languages, which is not the case for many populations). The important point here, however, is that when the English language is used as a marker of normal, then anyone who can't speak it is marked as abnormal—as being deficient or defective in some way. Even children who may arrive knowing several other languages are still considered deficient if they haven't yet learned English.

There is a rich, if troublesome, irony here: whereas many Americans consider it normal to speak only English and believe that they are incapable of learning a second language, they are impatient with people from other countries who arrive in the U.S. speaking only *their* native languages. Many Americans seem to expect anyone who sets foot in the United States to know English, or at least learn it immediately, despite the fact that Americans frequently travel to France without knowing French, to Italy without knowing Italian, and so on. And although many American adults often profess to be unable to learn another language at all, newcomer children are expected to master a new and difficult language with little or no difficulty and at breakneck speed. In expecting from children what they would not expect from themselves, many adults unfairly hold children from the outgroup *speakers-of-other-languages* to a standard they themselves might not even attempt.

Children, Language, and Identity

Interestingly, and again ironically, while many Americans define themselves as people who speak English and only English, they don't seem to recognize that children who arrive in this country also likely define themselves as people who speak a specific language. That is, newly arrived children identify with their mothers and fathers and brothers and sisters as Korean or Dominican or Rwandan or Gujarati, and so they think of themselves as someone who speaks Korean or Spanish or Kinyarwanda or Gujarati. Just as English is part of many Americans' identity, heritage languages are part of immigrant children's identities. People who react to non-English speakers by insisting "This is America—they should be speaking English" are insisting on something that is far more complex and daunting than they imagine.

Trying on a new identity is difficult for anyone, as discussed above. And, because language and nationality are critical components of our identity, the shift from one culture and identity to another is particularly difficult, as this young writer makes clear:

> I discovered the importance of defining myself when I came to Seattle. I remember one of my professors asked me where I came from and what language do I spoke. I said I came from Canada and I speak English and Chinese. And I will add one more sentence, "Originally, I came from Hong Kong and lived in Hong Kong for 11 years." I have struggled about what should I called myself. Who am I? I don't know what to say. Should I say I am Chinese-Canadian, or should I just say Chinese? I am mixed with all three nationalities: Chinese, Canadian, and American. At once point, I had tears, because I didn't know where I truly belonged.[5]

Such ingroup/outgroup confusion is extraordinarily painful because we all define ourselves in terms of group membership. In fact, the human need to belong is so strong that in his famous hierarchy of human needs, psychologist Abraham Maslow (1954) ranked only two things more important to humans than belonging: physiological needs (like food and water) and safety (being out of war zones, or being safe from abuse).[6]

And, adults need to know where they belong as much as children do. That the confusion exhibited by the young writer above may continue even into adulthood is obvious in the more mature writing of Enrique "Hank" López. Born in Bachimba, Mexico, the author came to the U.S. as a child and eventually graduated from Harvard Law School. After visiting Bachimba as an adult, López found that he could identify himself neither as American nor as Mexican, and that even the common term Mexican-American seemed an adequate marker of identity: "I, for one, am convinced that I have no true home, that I must reconcile myself to a schizo-cultural limbo, with a mere hyphen to provide some slight cohesion between my split selves" (1989, p. 239).[7]

For children, the formidable challenge of crafting a single identity from multiple parts is greater still when adults in the new culture signal to newcomer children who don't speak English that they have (and perhaps are) a problem. That is the case when their heritage language, which is so much a part of their first identity, is disregarded and devalued. Newcomer children are routinely told "Now that you're here, you have to speak English like us." Consider the implications of this message for children whose parents don't speak English: you have to speak English like us and get past the problem your (deficient) parents have. In many cases, accepting the need to learn and speak English means that the children also have to accept, consciously or not, the idea that there is something wrong with their parents and other family members—the people they most love in the world.

Yes, this is an oversimplification and yes, there are obvious, excellent reasons for newcomer children to learn English. But neither of those points negates the fact that in learning English, children are undertaking the difficult transition to a new culture and identity, as the bilingual authors cited above indicate. And, the process can become extremely painful if it works to erode family ties, as it often does. In fact, one of the most common reactions of children who learn English is to be ashamed of parents who don't speak it, or who don't speak it "correctly." For example, well-known author Amy Tan had this to say about herself as a girl:

> [W]hen I was growing up, my mother's "limited" English limited *my* perception of her. I was ashamed of her English. I believed that her English reflected the quality of what she had to say. That is, because she expressed them imperfectly her thoughts were imperfect. And I had plenty of empirical evidence to support me: the fact that people in department stores, at banks, and at restaurants did not take her seriously, did not give her good service, pretended not to understand her, or even acted as if they did not hear her. (2003, p. 134)[8]

Growing up in American society, Tan absorbed dominant language norms: the ability to speak "good" English as characteristic of people who are smart and deserve respect, and the inability to do so as characteristic of people who are not smart, not to be respected. Unhappily, these norms led Tan to be ashamed of her mother.

Perhaps if there were enough adult English classes for ELLs' parents so that they and their children might learn English simultaneously, the situation would be different (as it is for many ELLs whose parents do speak English). But many English classes for immigrant adults have long waiting lists, and families with few resources cannot afford private classes and tutors. Moreover, those parents who immigrated because of poverty are usually busy working multiple jobs to support their families, so that there is little or no time for learning a new language. When parents aren't learning the language, however, every step children take toward becoming English speakers is a step away from their families.

While non-English-speaking immigrant parents typically *want* their children to learn English, they often realize that it means the children will begin identifying with American culture, as Tan did above. That shift can, and often does, begin to fray the fabric of the family. Children becoming ashamed of their parents is only one of several potential problems. Siblings often begin conversing in English when they don't want their parents to know what they're talking about, for example, creating another type of ingroup/outgroup within the family unit. Moreover, children who become competent in English frequently become spokespersons for their parents in such common areas as stores and doctors' offices. In those situations, children become the experts, while parents must depend on their skills, turning the usual parent/child power relationship upside down.

Unlike learning how to count American money or which side of the road to watch when crossing the street, then, learning English is not a simple task for children either literally or emotionally. Instead, it is inextricably entwined with identity, with how they define themselves and which groups they are most comfortable in. And, advances in mastering English often come at the expense of family relationships. This is not to say schools should not teach newcomer students English, or those students shouldn't apply themselves to learning it. It is to say, however, that teachers should understand that the task goes far beyond simply learning that *mother* means *madre*, and they should consciously strive to be less judgmental and more patient as children begin moving toward an American identity.

Beyond Language

Language, clothing and food are among the most obvious markers of culture, allowing individuals to easily identify members of their ingroups and outgroups. Americans, for example, might easily identify a group of women as *not-American* if they were wearing burkas, or speaking Swahili, or snacking on giant water beetles. As the title of this chapter intends to suggest, however, less obvious norms saturate and influence many other areas of daily life. This is true outside of classrooms—but also within them, where unrecognized cultural norms can wreak havoc on the teaching/learning process.

Cultural Norms, Cultural Routines, Routine Conflicts

Cultural norms aren't simple ideas that people have about themselves: they are ideas that shape behavior. Taken together, they determine the patterns of our every day activities: what we wear, what we eat, but also what we say and do. To take the obvious examples above, a typical American woman doesn't wake up in the morning and decide not to wear a burka—the idea would never occur to her in the first place. Of course, she *could* wear it; there's nothing to stop her (though she might have to order it over the internet). But because no women in her in-groups wear one, she unconsciously absorbs the idea that she should not buy and wear that particular item of clothing—although many women in other cultures and places do. A cultural norm is operating any time any-one says something like "Why is he wearing *that?* Why is she doing *that?*" Cultural norms are behind what we hear so often: "That's *weird.*" What we forget is that the judgments *normal/weird* depend upon being in a particular place at a particular time. American women who think it normal to wear shorts would be judged harshly for doing so in a culture that places a high value on modesty—perhaps even considered crimi-nals for their weird clothing.

The burka/shorts examples are obvious ones, but cultural norms af-fect a wide swath of life, sometimes visibly, sometimes invisibly, but al-ways with influence over choices and patterns of behavior. Various religions, for example, influence what people do and don't eat, when they pray, how they pray, where they send their children to school—or perhaps whether they choose to homeschool them. Families, too, have an assortment of norms. One family might prioritize family gatherings so that anyone who skipped a family event would face the criticism, per-haps wrath, of relatives; another family might stress individualism and independence, so that rather than coming "home for the holidays," someone might instead go on safari without suffering family fallout. Age is another influential factor, with some activities (like wearing makeup or having a paid job) generally considered inappropriate for young American children and some (like participating in challenging physical activity) considered inappropriate for senior citizens. For example, the national press was agog when former president George H. W. Bush went skydiving to celebrate his 85th birthday because skydiving is just not something people in their 80s *norm*ally do.

It is impossible to list the many individual norms that govern daily life, or even all of their many sources: nations, families, religions, political groups, race, geography, socioeconomic status, job or profession, age, friends, education, role models...on and on and on. We can't be aware of each norm individually, in part because there are simply too many of them. In fact, because norms help make life more manageable by limiting the number of choices we have to think about consciously everyday, we're much better off being unaware of many of them—especially those that help us stay safe. After all, we don't want Americans consciously deciding which side of the road to drive on at any given *moment*; we want them to automatically steer toward the right without pondering the British alternative of steering left.

There are times, however, when *not* being aware of cultural norms causes problems because of the way humans assume *different* behavior is *abnormal* or *inferior* behavior. For example, communication scholar Deborah Tannen (1990) has detailed the many different communication norms American men and women exhibit and the issues that arise from the differences.[9] Men, she says, must talk all day in their work life, so that talk is a tool to get their own way, or to gain power over someone else, or to sell something, or to make something else happen in the world. Therefore, when men come home to a female partner, they assume *not talking* is a privilege in the relaxing world of home, a place where they don't have to be "on" every moment. But for women, Tannen says, talk is a sign of intimacy; in sharing secrets and stories of their daily lives, women create shared emotional space for their ingroups of friends and families. Women use talk to nurture and strengthen important emotional connections.

Given such different understandings of what it means to talk, it is no surprise that men and women argue about communication. Women judge men to be cold and distant if they offer one-word responses to questions like "How was work today?" ("Fine"), while men judge women to be unreasonably demanding (and perhaps even unable to just shut up) if they want to talk, talk, talk when the men are off duty. Women feel disrespected and excluded, men feel pressured, both become angry, and cold wars often ensue. Each gender assumes *its* preferred style of home communication to be obviously better than and preferable to the other— typical ingroup/outgroup behavior.

Again, of course, this is an overgeneralization (subgroups being what they are), but it illustrates the ways in which unrecognized norms lead us into daily conflicts and often escalating hostilities. Whether a particular battle ends in a shared laugh or leads to the door of a marriage therapist depends in part upon whether the participants can figure out what's happening and work toward a plan that meets both their needs. This pattern of unspoken (and often unconscious) assumptions leading to misunderstandings and conflicts is an everyday occurrence, and that is as true inside schools as outside of them.

Classroom Norms, Classroom Routines, Classroom Conflicts

Like the men and women described above, various cultures also have different norms for communication. For example, in many cultures children learn that it is disrespectful to look directly into the eyes of an authority figure, like a parent or teacher. In contrast, in American culture *not* looking at a speaker signals that the listener isn't paying attention, or perhaps is just plain rude. One of the most common classroom culture clashes happens, then, when an American teacher speaks directly to a newcomer student and that student refuses to look the teacher in the eye, instead keeping his or her eyes on the floor. Often, the American teacher reads the child's behavior negatively as extreme shyness or backwardness, or as disrespect. Like parents, angry teachers often insist "You look at me when I'm speaking to you!"

This obvious example is only one of several communication issues that crop up routinely in multicultural classrooms. And, communication itself is only one of several areas of classroom life where cultural misunderstandings frequently occur. The following discussion offers a brief overview of several potential problem areas, but readers should not consider it exhaustive. Instead, the segment points to a few areas where cultural norms frequently collide to alert teachers to how frequently unspoken norms vary and how easily misunderstandings can occur. Teachers need much deeper understanding of specific cultures than we can provide here; starting points for that type of learning appear later in this chapter and in the Appendix.

Communication and Body Language. Eye contact, as discussed above, is only one way that members of a culture signal respect for others. Many cultures have a strict hierarchical order, with children occupying the lower rungs and expected to be humble—and often quiet. It is not unusual for adults in other cultures to expect children to spend their days listening and learning from adults. Children from such cultures therefore tend to be quiet, and they hesitate to "bother" the teacher with questions. American teachers, however, generally expect children to ask questions if they are confused, or to participate in group discussions. For dutiful children who want to show the teacher total respect, complying with teacher requests for active student discussion and questioning can be extremely difficult, even painful. Too often, American teachers jump to the conclusion that silent children are uninterested, dull, or socially awkward.

Similarly, various cultures have norms for the distance between speakers in a conversation. In American culture, for example, most people are careful not to "invade" someone else's "personal space." Such invasion can be considered not only rude, but also aggressive (as when people go "nose to nose"). *Norm*ally, Americans stand back and a bit away from others when conversing (except, of course, for lovers—whose physical closeness communicates the nature of their relationship). In many other cultures, however, speakers stand much closer together. Until they have adjusted to American norms, children from such cultures may make their teachers and classmates uncomfortable by standing closer than expected.

Touching, too, can be misunderstood. In many cultures, members of the opposite sex are not allowed to touch—so that asking a boy and a girl to hold hands in a line might be a forbidden act for a newcomer, no matter how well intentioned the teacher's instruction to do so.

Even smiling or nodding can be misunderstood. While a smile generally signals happiness or approval to an American, in other cultures it may have far different meanings, including confusion or embarrassment. Or, as in Thai culture, a smile may indicate an apology. Imagine the reaction of a teacher who was scolding a Thai child for not following directions if the child simply smiled! Surely the poor child would be scolded still further for disrespect, or for not taking the teacher's comments seriously ("You think this is funny?"). Similarly, while nodding generally means "Yes, I understand, I agree" to an American, in other cultures it may simply mean "I'm listening."

And, of course, some topics which are assumed appropriate for public conversation in some cultures are taboo in others. These range from questions about a person's family to comments about politicians or monarchs.

Yet one more common communication glitch is what American teachers frequently consider a newcomer student's total inability to answer a question directly, or to write a simple topic sentence or thesis to guide a piece of writing. However, in many cultures, direct statements are considered rude, and topics are addressed indirectly, often with high value placed on poetic prose. Therefore, what is polite speech in one culture may equate to "beating around the bush" in another. Such differences in style can lead American teachers to incorrectly assume that students don't know answers or don't have clear ideas when they actually do—but are trying to be polite.

Teacher and Parent Roles. American educators expect that parents will be interested in their children and in their schools. The norms for parent behavior include contacting teachers with questions and concerns, responding to notes sent home, attending school events, and volunteering to help out in the classroom. As even many American parents complain, such norms often ignore the reality that many parents are themselves overscheduled with multiple jobs and responsibilities.

A first consideration here, then, is that parents may have so many other responsibilities that they simply do not have, and cannot make, time for school events or volunteering. They are not uninterested; they are simply *busy.* Even when parents might have time to contribute, and even in cases where they may speak English themselves, if they come from a culture where teachers are highly respected professionals who are never questioned, then parents may refrain from actively participating in a school discussion about solutions to problems or next steps in some area. As is true for their children, some parents may refrain from asking questions out of respect for the teacher and a desire not to be rude. This is true in Mexican culture, for example, where it is assumed that schools will teach academics (leaving the parents out of it) and families will teach values (leaving the school out of it). Many Mexican parents have little to say to teachers because they wouldn't dream of insulting them by having an opinion about classroom and school matters.

Of course, language can be a problem in relationships with non-English-speaking parents as well. If a note from school were to actually make it out of a child's backpack and into a parent's hand, what if there were no translator available (as there often is not)? If no one were available to tell the parent what the note said, then the parent would be unable to respond by sending an answer to a question, or by appearing at a scheduled conference. Again, educators might misread such gaps as disinterest on the part of the parent, who instead had no way to access information about what response was wanted.

Because the motivation for immigration is so often a desire for a better life for children, parents of newcomer children are generally (if not universally) highly supportive of education and stress its importance to their children. It's unfortunate and unhelpful that so often their lack of visibility *in* the school is misinterpreted as a sign of disinterest.

Values. Culture differences in values are easily illustrated by an activity once popular in American classrooms. During the time that "character education" was popular, this activity introduced a scenario where a small group of people were in some dire situation (stranded in an overcrowded lifeboat, for example), with one having to die so that the others might live. Students had to decide which person to sacrifice. Their choice always involved deciding who matters most in a society because the choices always involved representatives of various groups—children, mothers, religious leaders, and so on. What teachers quickly noticed was how often student responses could be predicted by their cultural backgrounds. Although Americans were extremely reluctant to sacrifice a child (*because her whole life lies ahead*), they often thought that sacrificing someone old was the best option (*because he's already had a full life*). Interestingly, many students who identified with other cultures— especially Asian cultures—would be extremely reluctant to sacrifice the elderly person. In direct contrast to the American view, other cultures often revere their elderly as precious sources of wisdom and consider them cultural treasures.

What is more valuable: youth or age? Book learning or practical skills? Sharing or conserving resources? Competing or cooperating? Predictability or adventure? Family or individuality? Honor or success?

The answers to such questions constitute a culture's value system, which is a critical source of cultural identity. Even among Americans, differences in subculture values cause conflicts in schools. Conservative parents, for example, are often dismayed at cooperative school projects, believing that to succeed in a capitalist economic system their children need instead to learn to compete. The opportunity for such value clashes multiplies substantively when teachers and students come from entirely different cultures. An American teacher may consider school attendance the highest priority a family could have for a child. However, if the home culture stresses shared sacrifice for family's welfare, a child might go willingly to work with a parent, helping to pick crops when the family is short on money for food. In such circumstances, choosing school over work would seem a terribly selfish act to the child.

What's a Teacher to Do?

Many education students who first become aware of the vast impact of culture in the classroom feel overwhelmed by all they don't know. They positively wail: "How am I supposed to know everything about every culture that might turn up in my classroom? I've got all this academic stuff to learn, and all these methods, and assessments and school rules and policies and standardized tests to worry about—how can anyone expect me to learn about every culture as well?" This is a reasonable but unwarranted and unhelpful response.

No one could possibly know every culture there is to know. That's not what is asked of teachers. Instead, teachers must remember that cultural differences have enormous impact on the classroom, and they must do their best to help newcomers begin the hard work of navigating a new culture. An obvious first step for teachers is to consciously resist their ethnocentric tendency to judge other cultures inferior and to resist projecting unfortunate stereotypes onto children. Most native Spanish-speaking students are not undocumented Mexicans, for example, and not every Asian child is a whiz at math. Immigrant parents are not all undocumented, or uneducated, or unable to speak English, or poor. Rather than making assumptions based on stereotypes, teachers need to learn about individual students and families who have become part of their communities.

In addition to avoiding stereotyping and assumptions of cultural inferiority, there are also positive steps teachers can take to help themselves and their students avoid the cultural miscommunications detailed above. Later chapters will explore specific language teaching strategies useful in working with ELLs, but there are preliminary steps teachers can take to bridge the cultural worlds of the newcomers' homes and their schools.

Use Multicultural Literature as Windows and Mirrors

Luckily, in recent years there has been an explosion of high-quality multicultural books for children and adolescents. Such books are useful to every member of the classroom community. A story reflecting the customs and values of a culture unfamiliar to classroom citizens (including the teacher) offers a "window" into a new world. Readers can learn about clothing, greetings, holidays, games, foods—even some common words and phrases. Such works are also valuable for children from the culture depicted, serving as a "mirror" where children can see themselves. Such mirrors offer the comfort of the familiar in the midst of an unfamiliar classroom world, creating a bridge between the world of home and the world of school.

The best multicultural literature illustrates both differences and similarities between cultures, so that differences are acknowledged even as similarities among students everywhere are highlighted. For example, while children may play different games in different cultures, all children enjoy playing games with their friends. Teenage girls may wear very different clothing in different cultures, but it's likely that they all enjoy sharing secrets with their friends. A multicultural group of students that comes to see each other as both different *and* the same can begin knitting itself into cohesive classroom community. Moreover, teachers who seek out multicultural books for their classrooms will inevitably learn a great deal about other cultures simply by exploring the possibilities.

A word of caution is in order, however. What is true of books in general is true of multicultural books: some authors are brilliant and do admirable work, while others jump on a commercial bandwagon and write anything that will sell. Unfortunately, some works depicting other cultures are misinformed, or they advance unhelpful stereotypes (perhaps by accident, but damage results anyway). This is true even for books that may have won prestigious awards. While a teacher unfamiliar with a culture can't be expected to spot inaccuracies, guidelines are readily available to help teachers make reasonable judgments about the merit of particular books. A simple internet search on guidelines or guides for selecting multicultural literature will yield a great deal of advice and help. Building a multicultural classroom library is one of the easiest and most effective steps a teacher can take to help head off cultural clashes.

Secondary teachers who think this advice applies only to elementary classrooms should think again. Picture books can be useful in a middle or high school, and every culture has its heroes who have contributed to disciplines like science and mathematics. If there are students from other cultures in the classroom, there is a way that multicultural literature can be useful to the teacher.

Make an Effort to Visit and Learn about the Students' Home Communities

While teachers routinely expect parents to visit the classroom, they far less routinely visit their students' home communities. While a home visit is often extremely useful, practical realities (like the parents' work schedules, or the teachers' concern about communicating in two entirely different languages) may make the teacher hesitant to attempt an in-person visit with the parents. In those cases, the teacher may still productively venture into the student's world. Browsing in community stores, eating in community restaurants, or attending community events (fairs, dances, religious celebrations) can provide a great deal of information about a community and its culture. And, the teacher may learn just enough to start conversations with students from the community and learn still more: "I saw a lot of dried fish in the store. Do you eat that often? In what kind of dishes?" Or, "I noticed that all the women were wearing a lot of very similar bracelets. Do they have some kind of meaning—are they for luck or something? Or are they just fashionable?"

Any new learning—picking up a word or two from a shopkeeper or a waiter, noting an unfamiliar dish on a menu, hearing a different type of music in the background—can lessen the sense of other cultures as unknown and *weird*. When we begin developing some familiarity with a new culture, we stop avoiding it. Instead, we begin adding some of its elements to what we already know and like: we begin eating falafel, or listening to K-pop, or yelling "¡Cállate!" at the dog. It is for this reason, for the possibility of finding new things we are glad to know about, that multicultural enthusiasts speak so often of the riches of a multicultural society.

Use the Internet

Given the world of information made readily accessible via computers, learning basics about other countries and cultures takes only a few keystrokes and a little bit of time. A simple search on a country will quickly provide an outline of its history, its politics, its geography, its culture, and so on. Not only maps and informational narratives are readily available, but so are music videos and artworks and virtual tours of museums. The possibilities for independent learning are limitless—which is why we have included a list of resources for teachers later in this book. Yes, teacher time is limited. However, computers are usually handy, and if most education students are honest, they could pare a few minutes every day from online social networking to begin building their intercultural knowledge and competence.

Summary

Culture is an important force in every life and in every classroom. Our identity is shaped by our many cultures, and it is human nature to assume our culture is superior to everyone else's, a trait known as *ethnocentrism*. As a result, we all have to make a conscious effort to avoid equating *different* with *abnormal* and to avoid making assumptions about individuals we don't know based on unfair and inaccurate stereotypes. Teachers in particular should avoid jumping to conclusions about students and their parents. Instead, they should strive to be patient with English language learners, who are faced not only with the challenge of learning a new language and fitting in with their new peers, but also with navigating changes in identity and perhaps new family relationships. In addition, teachers need to anticipate and try to avoid common cultural misunderstandings in a variety of areas, including communication styles, body language, appropriate roles for teacher and parents, and a wide range of values.

Because each child deserves an opportunity to learn, teachers are responsible for making classrooms safe and comfortable learning environments where differences are accommodated rather than denigrated. To shape such environments, they can take several positive steps, including: building multicultural classroom libraries to serve as cultural windows and mirrors; venturing into students' homes and/or home communities; and, using the internet to learn about the cultures represented by individual students in their classes.

Explorations

1. Even when students seem to closely resemble each other, their membership in various subcultures means they are likely to have significant differences as well. To uncover the diversity even in your teacher education classroom, bring to class three cultural artifacts—that is, three things that reveal something about important elements of your identity. Be prepared to share your artifacts in small group discussions and to identify surprises in what you learned about your classmates.

2. Research a culture represented in your home or school community. Learn about such elements as language/s, geography, religion, politics, art, and so on, and prepare a multimedia presentation that will familiarize your classmates with the culture. Be sure to point out similarities and differences between the culture you research and American culture—or your own culture, if you don't identify as American.

3. Identify at least one book that you can imagine being a useful addition to your classroom in the future. Take your time in seeking out the book, browsing among the resources listed in the appendix. Be prepared to identify the book, say why/how you think it would be useful, and how you decided it conforms to guidelines for *good* multicultural works.

4. Ask someone of a different faith or culture to accompany you to an unfamiliar religious ceremony. Attend the service, and write a reflection capturing how it felt to be in a different environment as well as the similarities and differences you noted—especially differences you found appealing.

Notes

1   Tajfel, H. (1970). Experiments in intergroup discrimination. *Scientific American, 233*(5), 96–102.

2   Tajfel, H. (1970). Experiments in intergroup discrimination. *Scientific American, 233*(5), 96–102.

3   Howard, G. (1999). *We can't teach what we don't know: White teachers, multiracial schools.* New York: Teachers College Press.

4   Sidanius, J., & Pratto, F. (1999). *Social dominance: An intergroup theory of social hierarchy and oppression.* Cambridge, UK: Cambridge University Press.

5   lemontree. (n.d.) Hyphenated identities: A long search journey. *Universal Journal: The Association of Young Journalists and Writers.* Retrieved from http://ayjw.org/print_articles.php?id=696640

6   Maslow, A. (1954). *Motivation and personality.* New York: Harper.

7   López, E. H. (1989). Back to Bachimba. In G. Colombo, R. Cullen & B. Lisle (Eds.), *Rereading America: Cultural contexts for critical thinking and writing* (pp. 232–240). New York: St. Martin's. (Work originally published 1965).

8   Tan, A. (2003). Mother tongue. In T. Cooley (Ed.), *The Norton Sampler* (6th ed., pp. 132–138). New York: Norton. (Originally published as "Under Western Eyes" in *The Threepenny Review*, 1990).

9   Tannen, D. (1990). *You just don't understand: Men and women in conversation.* New York: Morrow.

CHAPTER THREE

Language

You Know More—and Less—Than You Think

When our students digest the statistics of how many English language learners are in U.S. classrooms, and when they confront the fact that students in their classrooms are likely to include learners with no or minimal English language skills, their first reaction is usually tinged with alarm: "How am I supposed to relate to these kids if they can't understand what I say and I can't understand what they say?" They worry that they will not be able to have any real conversation with English language learners—let alone find ways to teach them new academic content. Their concerns usually stem from their belief that they know nothing at all useful that would help them meet these challenges. We believe, however, that pre-service teachers generally know much more about language than they think.

Let's take, for example, the question "What exactly do we mean when we use the term *language*?" To trigger thinking about that question, we sometimes show our students a video clip of a dog howling and ask: "Does that howling constitute a language?" Many students say yes, because the dog howls as a means of communication, just as humans use language. The howling signals to others such messages as "Danger!" or "I need company" or "I don't like it here." Other students argue that no, the howling is not a language, because human communication systems are different in essential ways (the use of words, for example) from non-human communication systems. What is interesting, however, is that whichever position they take on the howling question, students always recognize that the central feature of language is communication. That is, despite their disagreement about the forms language may take, they all correctly define language as a system for communicating thoughts, information or ideas. And, that's true whether we have an external audience or are just talking to ourselves, using our unspoken words or informal jottings to figure out what we think. As someone famous once said: "How do I know what I think until I see what I say?"[1] In other words, talking to yourself is still talking.

So our students are right: language is a communication system. That's a serviceable if not exactly sophisticated definition that will serve our purposes here. And, it's only the first of many things readers are likely to know about language, even if they aren't consciously aware of what they know. For example, the next segment discusses the interrelatedness of language, perceptions and power; we believe readers will be able to provide examples from their own experience once their awareness has been triggered.

Other information, however, is likely to be new: what it means to *know* a word; how oral and written language differ; how first and second languages develop; and, which elements of structure in the English language is essential for teachers to know. Unhappily, based on our experience we think that the structure of English is an area where most readers should recognize content (the definition of a *noun* and a *verb*, for example)—but that too many will not. Although our students report that they underlined zillions of verbs in grade school, they also report being stymied when we ask them to identify the subject and verb in a sentence. While our overview of English language structure cannot be exhaustive, given the scope of this text, we trust it will at least provide a blueprint for further study if readers find themselves at a loss to understand the material.

Language: Facets, (Mis)Perceptions, and Power

In this segment we explore how both verbal and non-verbal elements shape spoken messages to help listeners understand a speaker's intentions. Such information will be useful in understanding how adults help babies develop language. We look, too, at the way that the particular form of a message can cause some audiences to leap to some misunderstandings about the speaker—a habit that teachers working with ELLs must guard against, as we've cautioned before and will caution again.

Facets of Human Language

While words are obviously central to messages, they are only part of our overall communicative strategies. To be specific, when we want to use language to accomplish something, we routinely consider the context (or situation) we're in and the content (or meaning) we want to represent, and then we choose appropriate linguistic expressions (like words or sentences). These factors are what linguist Edward Finnegan (1994) [2] calls the "three faces of language." To oversimplify just a bit, those faces are: context, (what is the situation?), content (what meaning is intended?), and linguistic expression (which words are used?). For example, a teenager answering the question "What did you do last night?" is likely to include different details and use different vocabulary depending upon whether the person who asked the question is a parent or a good friend. An answer to a parent is not likely to contain vulgar expressions or details about being chased by the police. In contrast, an answer to a friend might well be laced with lusty language and contain an excited and detailed account of the police chase. No doubt readers have been similarly selective in conversations with significant others in their own lives.

So far, so good. Now, to think a little more deeply about the relationship between context and content, consider the following scenario. Assume that during a dinner at home, a parent asked a teenager sitting at the other end of the table to pass the salt and pepper:

Parent: Could you pass me the salt and pepper?

Teenager: No.

Actually, we can't tell what content, or what message, either the parents or the teenager intended or communicated here because we can't see the situation. That is, we don't know enough about the context.

If the family were seated at a large table, the parent might have been asking whether the salt and pepper were within the teen's reach; after checking, the teen might have said "No," indicating the shakers were too far away. The content in this case would be information about the physical location of the salt and pepper. Or, the table might have been relatively small and the salt and pepper might have been directly in front of the teen. In this case, the response "No" would indicate the teen's unwillingness to offer the parent the smallest bit of cooperation, for whatever reason. The words alone cannot tell us either which question the parent intended or what the teen meant by his response. Although we rarely say to ourselves "Now, what's the context of this message I'm about to send?" we all routinely adapt our messages to different audiences and purposes—making the students reading this book likely masters of contextual adaption, even if they aren't aware of it. As will be obvious shortly, context is a key consideration for any language learner.

Now, let's think about words just a bit more, because while they're obvious, they also have important implications. When a child in the United States or other English-speaking country is thirsty (context) and understands what water means (content), she can use the word to ask for water.

Child (approaching her mom washing dishes): Water!

Mom (opening a cupboard to retrieve a cup): Okay.

In this example, the sound of w-a-t-e-r is an English expression that represents the clear liquid we drink to quench thirst. However, if the child and mom were in Korea, the child would use a different linguistic expression, m-oo-l, which represents the same meaning in a similar conversational context. The same content can be signaled using very different sounds, a point that is most obviously demonstrated by comparing words for the same thing in two or more languages.

Interestingly, however, the point about different words being used in different contexts is not limited to different languages. For example, different dialects—or variations of a single language—frequently use different words to describe the same thing. Soft drinks are called *Coke* in the Southern part of United States, while *pop* is used in Michigan, and *soda* in the Eastern United States. Dialects are often common to geographic regions, as in this example, but specific subcultures may also have less common dialects. For example, some people of Irish heritage say "Jay-sus" when speaking the word most Americans pronounce "Jee-sus" (Jesus). And, some people might say "He ain't rich" while others would say "He isn't rich," but both obviously mean the same thing.

Since it's often possible to determine intended meaning even when specific terms or pronunciations vary (thanks in part to context), linguists often assert that no one dialect or language is inherently superior to any other. When a language seems inadequate to convey all of the messages its users want to send, the users simply adopt new words or other forms of expression and expand the language. For example, the expressions "I Googled it" or "Did you see that Tweet about the rave?" have only recently become intelligible linguistic expressions in the United States; they were added as efficient ways to indicate specific content that users wanted to include in their communications. Because languages grow with the needs of their users, they are all equally effective. It is for this reason, in fact, that as we opened this chapter we specifically selected a definition of *language* broad enough to include Pidgin English, Pig Latin, English and French; each is capable of bearing all the messages that the people using it wish to send, and so no one language or dialect is inherently superior to another as a communication system.

The point here is one that linguists make over and over, a crucial point that bears repeating: all dialects and languages meet the needs of their language communities, and no single language or dialect is inherently superior to another. Unfortunately, few people have studied linguistics. As a result, they frequently, and inappropriately, consider language variations to be markers of outgroups—groups inferior to their own. And this, of course, has implications for English language learners and their families.

Language and (Mis)Perceptions

Having lived in various states in our lives, we have friends who are from or are living in many parts of the United States. Therefore, our friends speak many regional dialects. As they have moved from place to place, some of them have experienced insensitive remarks about their language habits. For example, one of our friends who grew up in the South moved with his wife to the West Coast for a decade. They became members of a church, and during one leisurely lunch hour following a Sunday service, a local church member asked our friend if his wife thought as slowly as she talked. The remark was likely intended as a joke, but it alerted the couple to the fact that others in the community viewed their dialect negatively. The incident was a painful one for the Southerners, and it left an indelible impression on them. Such judgmental comments are jarring for those who receive them, but unfortunately jokes about speakers of different dialects are common in the United States. Members of one subculture frequently perceive the dialect of other subcultures as *weird* and perceive its speakers as inferior in intelligence or ability or in any number of other ways.

While it is useful in many ways to be able to perceive similarities and differences among people—that is, to be able to identify ingroups and outgroups—that ability is a mixed blessing. Perceptions of sameness let us feel connected, grounded, safe and comfortable, which is important to our physical and mental well-being. However, when we assign superiority to our ingroups (consciously or not) based on language use, we often leap to unfounded and inaccurate perceptions of others.

Speaking slowly does not reflect limited ability to think, as assumed in the example above. Speaking quickly does not reflect rudeness, as Southerners often assume of Easterners in the United States. Speaking loudly does not reflect aggressiveness, as many people assume when a herd of noisy male adolescents makes its boisterous way down a sidewalk. And, saying "He ain't rich" is no barometer of intelligence, because anyone who grew up speaking English knows exactly what that means— even though many listeners would quickly dismiss this speaker as stupid based on the use of the word *ain't.*

English language learners are often disadvantaged by this common misperception that if people don't speak or write in a form that conforms to what they consider *Standard English*, they are uneducated or unintelligent. In fact, our students often insist that only Standard English should be taught or allowed in schools. Asked to define it, they will say things like it is basic or foundational English, book language, the language of television news programs, or language free of slang, dialects and other impurities. Linguists, however, inform us that there is no Standard English in the United States because the country has no official committee or process charged with defining and maintaining standards for American English. Instead, what Americans tend to call Standard English is actually just one more dialect—which happens to typically be spoken by Americans with a good bit of power and privilege. (And, for that reason, some cynics refer to it as "cash English.") It is indeed the dialect of the nightly news, but that doesn't make it the only "correct" English—simply the dialect most often spoken in some privileged contexts and the one enforced in classrooms, especially in written work.

Many people also mistakenly believe that what they call Standard English is the dialect of English that is spoken around the world. This too is a myth. While English is a popular language, the particular form spoken in any one country is likely to differ significantly from that spoken elsewhere. Language rules, enunciation, and word choices, among many other linguistic characteristics, evolve in speech communities. This makes sense, because geography affects language development. If people living in the southern United States developed different dialects from those living in Brooklyn or Boston, there is no reason to expect speakers in the U.S., Great Britain, Ireland, India and Africa to sound exactly alike. Indeed, there is a name for the various forms of English spoken internationally: *World Englishes*. And, it's useful to remember that English is used widely not because it is inherently superior to other languages, but because of British imperialism and U.S. military and economic domination on the world stage. As is implied in the above discussion of high-prestige dialects, language and power are inextricably intertwined, as we'll discuss in more detail below.

The habit of assigning negative characteristics to those who speak other dialects or languages poses a great challenge for English language learners. When people who learned to speak English from birth, including teachers whose first language is English, find that they cannot communicate with English language learners, too often they wonder whether the ELLs have any mental ability at all. If a teacher gives what she perceives as a simple command ("Look at your book") and an English language learner stares back blankly, too often the teacher is exasperated by what she perceives as the student's lack of intelligence and ability.

But remember: language is a communication system. And, classroom communication involves two parties, a sender and a receiver. Therefore, when communication fails, both parties likely bear responsibility. While the sender must consider context and other elements of a message and try her best to make it comprehensible to others, the receiver bears an equal responsibility to try to understand the message the sender intends, even if it is phrased in an unusual, imperfect or incomplete way. If a toddler says "Water," for example, the mother routinely helps communication by inferring the rest of the sentence and responding, "Oh. Would you like a glass of water?" In cases where the speaker is inexpert for any reason, listeners can facilitate communication by at least trying to infer meaning from context.

That reality is too rarely recognized in U.S. classrooms full of English speakers, who are confident in their own linguistic ability but lacking practice in shaping messages for an audience unfamiliar with the language or in applying themselves to understanding messages phrased in unusual ways. Rather than making a special effort to design messages that ELLs can at least partially comprehend, fluent English speakers most often assume that the communication problem can be alleviated only by ELLs learning English. That is, the entire burden for effective communication is typically placed on ELLs, which multiplies the challenges of American classrooms for them. Instead, teachers need to be more thoughtful in how they communicate with ELLs, and more patient in trying to understand the messages they send. We'll talk more about strategies for crafting intelligible messages in the next chapter, but in general what we're suggesting here is that teachers need to be sensitive to what learners do and don't understand about English and to consciously model various features of the language. By doing so, they rightly assume some of the responsibility for making classroom communication work and helping students develop increasing mastery of the language.

Language and Power

As we suggested above when we pointed out that too often teachers assign all responsibility for classroom communication to ELLs, language dominance bestows power. Those who speak the dominant language have no need to accommodate speakers of other languages, whereas speakers of minority languages face a great deal of pressure to learn the majority language.

For example, we have a friend who moved to the United States from Canada, which is a bilingual country where citizens speak both English and French. She visits her mother and other family members in Canada frequently, and returning from one of these visits, she described her mother's complaints about French speakers in her town. As a speaker of English, the mother could not function in certain areas of the town where French speakers were in the majority. Even though she was in her own country, each time she visited the French-dominant part of town she felt as if she were living in a foreign country because French speakers expected English speakers to communicate in French. Because she had grown up speaking English, she felt powerless and thought the French-speaking townspeople extremely unfair. While the country is officially bilingual, in some regions French is dominant, in others English, so that Canadians who are not themselves bilingual can feel as if they are visiting a foreign country as they move from one part of town, or from one province, to another.

This, however, is a stark contrast to the United States, where English is the language spoken by the majority, and there is no expectation that anyone will speak any other language. Thus, immigrants who speak languages other than English are often made to feel inadequate when they speak their home languages. Like the Canadians who venture from one language-dominant area to another, non-English speakers in the United States are similarly expected to speak the language being spoken to them. Like our friend's mother, they are often frustrated when speakers of the dominant language make no effort to help establish communication. The power of one group over the other is unspoken, but no less real: the person who wants the job, or who wants to know where to find something, or who wants to know how to get somewhere—or who wants to learn something in school—is the person whose needs aren't met when communication fails. They are the ones disadvantaged in such situations. It is precisely because language and power are linked that people who speak a dominant language so often resist the use of other languages.

Aware that they are a language-minority outgroup, aware that they are different, English language learners often feel uncomfortable in classrooms. Even in schools where teachers and students welcome newcomers, ELLs often stand alone in a corner of the school playground during recess. Like the English-speaking Canadian frustrated when she couldn't communicate with the clerk in a French-dominant part of town, English language learners can become frustrated when they cannot respond to the teacher's questions, even if they know the answers. Sometimes, they act out to compensate for the discomfort of being in a place where they cannot communicate with most of their classmates. In short, ELLs often feel powerless, even though their English-speaking classmates may not feel more powerful. Their inability to communicate in English prevents them from participating in class activities and having any control in their learning environment.

Again, having English-speaking peers and classroom teachers assume a greater share of responsibility for communication would do much to help ELLs engage with the classroom community and develop English proficiency. Such support is crucial, especially for ELLs who live in a home community where little or no English is spoken.

Language Development

To design strategies to help students acquire a new language, it's important for teachers to understand how language skills develop. Linguists, philosophers, psychologists and others have long been captivated by the question "How do people develop language?" Their work has generated volumes of research, but typically little of what they've found has filtered down to teachers. Unfortunately, researchers tend to write in language accessible only to other researchers (another example of members of one group refusing to shape messages in a way that allows members of other groups to understand them). As a result, teachers and education students, and sometimes even experienced researchers, may find reading research on language development difficult and frustrating.[3]

We certainly can't summarize everything that's known here. What we can and will do, however, is sketch key lessons for teachers that emerge from the research about language and language acquisition and discuss their implications for the classroom. Some additional thinking about what it means to know a word is a good place to start, since words are a key building block in language development. It's important, too, to consider the differences between oral and written language. As we'll discuss, those differences reaffirm the importance of context and offer some insight into differences between first and second language acquisition. Then, with this foundation in place, we'll outline first and second language development.

Knowing a Word

When we say that we *know* a word, we actually mean that we have mastered three aspects of it. The first aspect is real world knowledge, which is often knowledge of a tangible object (a ball or crib, for example) but which also includes understanding of concepts (what we mean by *love*, for example). The second aspect is knowledge of oral language, that is, the sounds of an object's name. And the third aspect is knowledge of written language, or how the spoken word is represented graphically. Because English has a sound-based (phonetic) writing system, it requires users to have knowledge of letters or clusters of letters that represent the sounds of an object's name. For example, when we say we know the English word *water*, it means that we know the clear liquid we drink when we are thirsty. We also know the sounds and written letters signaling w-a-t-e-r.

Word knowledge develops as young children interact with adults and surroundings. As adults identify objects around them, young children are exposed to words that can communicate their needs and wants to parents and other caregivers. A single word can carry a key message. Without uttering a full sentence, for example, a child can say "Water!" to express the idea, "I want water." Parents and other caregivers understand the child's intended meaning based on their knowledge of both the child and the context. As they mature, children gain new knowledge of the world and expand their vocabulary to include new words, including the words' sounds and graphic representations. Obviously, if a mature language speaker can point to a concrete object in the world while saying its name (ball), it is easier for a language learner to associate the word with its meaning.

As Michael Tomasello (2003)[4] has pointed out, word knowledge is central to language learning. English language learners, like other language learners, must develop word knowledge if they are to function effectively in new learning environments. For example, ELLs who understand and can say the word bathroom can tell teachers a great deal about what they need at a given moment. There are many other essential words like lunch, pencil, paper and homework that can help them successfully navigate the school environment. What teachers need to remember is that being able to say the word, or to read the word, is not enough: they must master all three aspects—meaning, pronunciation and spelling. As ELLs work to navigate the classroom, they need classroom teachers to provide active help in building the vocabulary they need for various activities and lessons. And, they need teachers to monitor their progress by checking to be sure they have mastered all three aspects of a word. Where teachers find gaps in understanding, they need to provide explicit instruction to help the student gain full mastery. Teachers who work with ELLs to help them continuously expand their vocabulary will improve their students' ability to function in the classroom environment, concurrently making that environment less threatening and more comfortable for them.

Oral Language vs. Written Language

We often believe that written language is simply oral language written down, but they are not the same. To communicate a message in a conversation, we supplement our words with facial expressions, gestures, tone of voice and other non-linguistic tools that linguists call *illocutionary forces*. The complete meaning of what we say is rarely found only in our words, as we demonstrated earlier in discussions of the importance of context. In our earlier discussion, we considered how the physical environment (the size of the table and location of the salt shaker) would give us essential clues to the meaning of the words spoken. Here, we want to think a bit more about what non-verbal tools speakers use to give listeners clues to meaning—because these tools can be particularly helpful to teachers trying to shape messages that ELLs can comprehend.

We pretty much use these non-linguistic tools without thinking about them, but their importance becomes obvious when we consider the difference between oral transcripts (which rely nearly exclusively on the words of a conversation) and written transcripts (which provide a great deal more information about non-linguistic, contextual information). Here are two examples that illustrate this point. Both were written by twelve-year-old Susan (who is bilingual, having learned both Korean and English as a child) depicting her experience ordering in a fast food restaurant. We feel confident readers will make allowances for her small mistakes as a bilingual, as we would for small mistakes made by any English-speaking twelve-year-old, so we haven't corrected them. This is Susan's oral transcript:

Cashier: Hello! Welcome to Wendy's. Is this for here or to go?

Susan: Here.

Cashier: Okay. And what would you like to order, ma'am?

Susan: (timidly) Umm, I'd like to order one small vanilla Frostie. (Adds in quickly) Please!

Cashier: Anything else? (looks up from cash register)

Susan: Uh, uh, yes. (Straightens and voice is more confident) One small decaf coffee, please.

Cashier: That'll be $1.98, ma'am.

(Susan hands two one-dollar bills to the cashier.)

Although the gestures and movements described in parentheses offer some additional information on the nature of the interaction, the reader still can gain only a vague sense of what actually transpired between Susan and the counter person.

Notice how much more we can understand about the encounter when Susan provides more information on non-linguistic signals in this written transcript, especially in terms of body language and tone:

> Susan walked up to the line and stood patiently behind a customer. He was a bit bulky as she thought studying him. As he walked away carrying his tray of food, Susan walked up to the cashier and smiled warmly. However, the cashier did not greet her with a smile, nor did he look happy. He simply stood there with a bored look plastered across his already stern face. "Hello. Welcome to the Wendy's. Is this for here or to go?" Susan replied, "Here." The cashier seemed to study the cash register. His fingers quickly danced upon the cash register. "Okay. And what would you like to order, ma'am?" Timidly, Susan looked up the dollar menu, trying to choose from cheeseburgers to chili's. "Umm, I'd like to order one small vanilla Frostie." She quickly added in, "please" before she completed her order. Once again, the cashier pressed different buttons and looked up as he asked, "Anything else?" She began to fool around with the embroidered moose on the left bottom corner of her shirt. "Uh, uh, yes." She let go of the moose and straightened, "One small decaf coffee, please." The cashier pressed buttons and replied, "That'll be $1.98, ma'am." Susan pulls out two one-dollar bills and hands them to him.

The written transcript of the conversation includes the same spoken words as the oral language transcript. However, additional information in the written transcript helps the reader understand Susan as a tentative customer eager to be polite and somewhat unsure of herself (*stood patiently*; *smiled warmly*; *quickly added in "please"*; *began to fool around with the embroidered moose on the left bottom corner of her shirt*). The clerk becomes someone whose body language suggested he had no interest in anything but completing the order—certainly not in welcoming this young woman to the establishment and helping her feel comfortable there (*did not greet her with a smile, nor did he look happy*; *bored look plastered across his already stern face*; *seemed to study the cash register*; *fingers danced quickly on the cash register*). The additional information on non-linguistic signals makes the encounter read more like a story, something we can see happening.

In discussions of this transcript and others like them, our students are quick to realize and offer examples of how much context contributes to understanding in a conversation. To take an obvious example, the words "Shut up!" can signal a threat, teasing, or surprise. Without knowing—at a minimum—the speaker's facial expression, stance and tone of voice, it would be impossible to tell what message the speaker intended. The implications for the classroom seem obvious: teachers need to supplement their words with multiple non-linguistic (illocutionary) signals—facial expressions, gestures, miming, and so on—in order to help students get some sense of what they are saying. Teachers who offer such contextual clues help ELLs bridge the vocabulary gap and better understand the classroom. Of course, in promoting understanding of their words, they also help ELLs expand their vocabulary.

First Language Development

English speakers who learned English in the earliest years of their lives rarely recognize the complex process they went through—just as they are rarely consciously aware of how much they rely on context to understand the spoken word. Perhaps the easiest way to call conscious attention to the many factors that help babies grow into competent language users is an example of what happens when those things we take for granted are missing. Linguists frequently use the story of Genie Wiley, also known as the "wild child," to illustrate some things researchers believe about language development. Genie spent her first twelve years locked in her bedroom. When she was identified and rescued, she was unable to speak. Intrigued by her case, many linguists made several ingenious attempts to teach her English, which should have been her first language. None of their efforts were successful: she never learned to speak at an age-appropriate level.

Many linguists consider Genie's story strong support for ideas articulated by Eric Lenneberg (1969), [5] who hypothesized that language development is a process that includes a critical period very early in life. Genie's difficulty with language may be due to the fact that she had been deprived of a normal environment during a critical point in the language development process, which would have occurred well before her twelfth year.

However, other factors may have also contributed to her inability to learn. For example, it seems impossible that she could have escaped severe emotional damage. Not only was she locked in her bedroom, she was also tied to a chair and punished whenever she uttered any sound. She never interacted with anyone except her parents, who brought food to her bedroom. Twelve years of such isolation is hard to imagine—and their impact on a growing child even more so.

While the "wild child" story is fascinating (you may want to read a detailed account online), we don't need to worry specifically about whether or not it confirms evidence of a critical period for language acquisition. What makes the story interesting in other ways is that it provides evidence for other elements of language development linguists have identified. Decades of research have demonstrated that language development is a process, and how babies grow into speakers of a language is well known. Genie would have been deprived of many factors researchers have identified as necessary for language development: extensive exposure to the language to be learned, competent speakers who serve as models and mentors, and real world experience and meaningful interaction.

As many readers may well know from experience, babies begin attempting language with cooing sounds. Their early cooing in the crib amounts to play and experimentation with various sounds, which helps them learn the range of sounds they can make. Very early on, however, they learn to discriminate between sounds used in the language spoken around them and sounds they do not hear in the environment—and like little geniuses, they abandon efforts to make sounds they don't hear. Soon, they are babbling—but babbling sounds they hear in their environment: muh-muh-muh or bah-bah-bah.

Adults help them develop their ability to form words by instinctively encouraging repetition of sounds that constitute words in the language being learned. In English, for example, babies are frequently coaxed to say ma-ma, or da-da. This helps explain why the first words of American babies with English-speaking parents are often *mama* or *dada.* Not only do parents have an inherent interest in teaching their children how to name them, but *mama* and *dada* are a fairly short step from their babbling experiments. They advance to using one and then two word combinations to communicate ("water!" "cookie!" "up sky!"), which linguists refer to as *telegraphic speech.*[6] What seems clear is that babies must hear the language they need to learn in order to discriminate its sounds, and they must have interaction with adults or other caregivers who listen to their cooing, babbling, and uttering of nonsensical words. Caregivers must also make an effort to understand them based on their knowledge of the babies and the context, and they must respond appropriately to their communicative intent (demonstrating that language is one way humans have to make things happen in the world).

From then on, it is also critical for babies to have things to point out, play with and talk about so that they can name these things with the help from adults or other caregivers, expanding their spoken vocabulary. Gradually, they add more details in messages to their caring listeners ("plane up sky!"), so that their utterances gradually lengthen. Listeners often help at this stage both by responding to the child's intended message and by modeling a more complete linguistic form of the message ("Yes. There is a plane up in the sky!") Because babies learn to speak so quickly, and because so much of the help they receive is instinctive (with mothers responding to "water" by handing off a cupful, for example), few people realize how much help competent speakers provide without either intending to or noticing that they have. In fact, language acquisition is so instinctual and so fast that adults who have never had extended interaction with babies may perceive them just as one theorist suggests: newly arrived from heaven and already talking. [7]

Second Language Development

An understanding of first language development lays the groundwork for understanding second language development, since it allows for comparisons and contrasts. Not surprisingly, the process of developing a second language may be somewhat different for different people. A constellation of factors, including age and first language, can make a significant difference in outcomes.

For example, a child born into a Korean-speaking family in the U.S. may very well learn English well enough to sound exactly like other people who were born into an English-speaking family and community. This might happen if the child had many interactions in the community with others whose first language was English, providing ample opportunity to listen and to practice speaking.

However, in different contexts the outcome might be very different. You might think, for example, that anyone who learned English at an early age might have no accent and sound just like someone whose first language was English. But that would not necessarily be the case. We have a friend whose first language was not English, but who was sent at an early age to an English-speaking country because his parents wanted him to learn a second language as a competitive advantage later in his life. However, as events turned out, his English skills were not as developed as others who had learned English in his home country where English was *not* widely spoken. At the same time, he didn't develop his home country's language proficiently, either. Former Secretary of State Henry Kissinger and his brother also provide examples of how much variance there can be among second language learners, even after they are immersed in the second language for extended periods of time. Although Kissinger immigrated to the United States during his teenage years and lived there for decades afterwards, he spoke with a strong German accent despite the fact that his sentences were always flawlessly structured. We learned that his brother's speech, however, had no trace of a German accent.

Accents are not dependable indicators of degrees of language fluency, but there are some characteristics of language use that can reveal challenges a speaker is working through as she develops a second language. The following discussion provides a glimpse of predictable difficulties ELLs may face. Again, however, we remind readers this is an introductory text. There is much more to be learned from independent reading, additional coursework, visiting immigrant communities and talking to people with diverse cultural and linguistic backgrounds.

Influence of the First Language

As a way to navigate a world overflowing with details, humans routinely try to use what they already know to understand something new. For example, a person who tasted a tomato for the first time might think "Ah. Something from the garden. It's not sweet. This must be a vegetable." Such thinking often works well to help us understand new phenomena and experiences—but certainly not always. According to biologists, for example, tomatoes are fruits; we call them vegetables because their taste (not sweet) puts them in the category of vegetables as far as cooks are concerned. This is pretty much the pattern of our daily experience: we use what we already know to make sense of new things, and sometimes it works, sometimes it partly works, and sometimes we're just wrong.

Much the same thing happens when second language learners use something they know about their first language in their attempts to use a new language. Consider, for example, the following question that Yonsu, a 12-year-old from Korea, asked of Meredith, her English as a Second Language (ESL) teacher. Yonsu was in the process of getting a letter ready to send to her grandparents in Korea and wanted to know if she could include a sticker with her letter.

Yonsu: Can I sticker put in here?

We can gain a few interesting insights from this question. Younsu correctly uses English vocabulary words and sentence structure she has already learned. However, it's hard not to notice that she placed the object of the verb, sticker, before the verb phrase, put in. Here, Yonsu uses what she knows about Korean in deciding where to put the word sticker, which is the object of the verb. In Korean, the object always comes before the verb, even in questions. Such errors are common, and teachers who pay attention to patterns in ELLs' writing can frequently see how the structure of a first language influences learners' use of the second language. While teachers will need to help students correct such mistakes, they should remember that many mistakes may be evidence of learners trying to master English by using what they know in their first language.

Teachers skilled in working with ELLs would likely also stop to think about Yonsu's use of "Can I." Although that phrase is part of daily language for most English-speakers, it's possible that Yonsu was using it in her speech more like a single word than a subject-verb combination. Research tells us that second language learners frequently learn common phrases (or "prefabricated chunks"[8]) and use them as if they were a single word before they understand that each of the words in the combination has a separate function in English. Only after they develop this deeper understanding do they begin to vary their use of the phrase. Evidence that Yonsu may have been using "can I" as a prefabricated chunk comes from other patterns in her writing. For example, she repeatedly wrote "I went to" in her home journal as she recorded places she and her family visited. It was nearly a month before she began to vary the phrase by saying "my family went to," indicating that she eventually recognized that "I" wasn't the only word that could be used with the verb phrase "went to." Similarly, Yonsu's use of "can I" as a chunk was visible in her home journal. After she took a jump rope to school for recess, her classmates were anxious for a turn. Discussing the event in her journal, she filled an entire page with utterances that included the phrase "Can I try?" The entry suggested that Yonsu was excited not only by the attention from her classmates, but also by her acquisition of a new English phrase.

The point we hope readers will take away from this discussion is that while the development of a first language tends to follow a fairly predictable path, there are many detours possible along the way for those who learn English as a second language. The above discussion describes two common issues: inappropriately applying rules from the first language, and mistakenly believing that two discrete words in a common phrase are inseparable and invariable. First language acquisition may be faster because it involves fewer opportunities to generate such errors, whereas detours during second language development may slow down efforts to demonstrate mastery.

Yet, there are many similarities in the processes. Both first and second languages seem to develop in progression. As in first language development, English language learners move from simple words combined with gestures to increasingly complex sentences eventually containing more and more detail. This progression, however, depends upon extensive opportunity to hear English being spoken in a variety of contexts and to engage in speaking, reading and writing English. Such a supportive learning environment with appropriate feedback on performance is key to both first and second language development.

One caveat is essential here: there is an enormous difference between learning to speak English conversationally and using it as a tool to master academic content. The latter is known to linguists as Academic English, or Cognitive Academic Language Proficiency (CALP).[9] Simply stated, CALP is the language spoken in classroom contexts, and it is different from informal English or Basic Interpersonal Communication Skills (BICS). For example, many of the nouns of conversational English correspond to things the learner can see, like *jump*, *desk* or *teacher*. However, the language of the classroom tends to be far more abstract and to require the understanding of ideas more than things: *compare*, *different* or *main point*. The fact that a child can be an active participant in conversations on the playground does not mean that she has developed the sophisticated understanding of English necessary to succeed in school. It is important for teachers to remember that a child who can converse comfortably in English may still need extra help understanding academic language and ideas. Researchers estimate that while it takes some three to five years for children to master conversation, it takes some four to seven years for them to master academic language, even when schools are doing a good job of meeting their need for accommodation.[10]

The Least Teachers Need to Know about English

When in our classes we begin to discuss the structure of English language, we find that our students often feel adrift. Despite having spoken English from birth, they often report hating that "English grammar stuff" while they were in grade school and insist that they don't know—and don't care to learn—what nouns, verbs, and adjectives are. As long as they have internalized rules and are not making egregious errors in their speech and writing, many students may indeed have experienced little need to understand formal terminology and the information it represents.

However, teachers don't have that luxury. If they can't articulate some basic features of the English language, they won't be able to help ELLs understand what they need to know. For example, while any teacher would recognize that Yonsu's question about the sticker was inappropriately worded, a teacher who didn't know that in English objects come after verbs would be of little help to her. To say to a student "That's wrong. Say it *this* way"—without explaining why—is likely to frustrate rather than help the English language learner. Students need to know not only how to make a particular sentence correct, but how to avoid the same error in future sentences. Because teachers can't teach what they don't know, they have to master at least some basic information about the English language.

Again: this is an introductory text and there is much more to know than the distilled information we offer here. We therefore urge readers to dust off the handbooks from their English composition classes and make an effort to learn more.

Lexical Categories

To explain why it's fine to say things one way in English but not fine to say them another way, teachers need first a good understanding of parts of speech, or *lexical categories*. These categories explain the different functions that words serve in English. For example, the subject of a sentence is most often a *noun*, and a teacher who doesn't know what a noun is would be hard-pressed to explain why "Mama cooks" is a sentence, but "Went fast" is not.

There are eight lexical categories: nouns, verbs, pronouns, adjectives, adverbs, determiners, prepositions and conjunctions. Nouns name persons, places, things and ideas (like *love*), and verbs are most often action words. These are the two types of words that students will encounter most frequently as they read. Detailing every category is beyond the scope of what we can accomplish here, but as a token reminder to students who may have some information on parts of speech buried deeply in their long-term memory, we offer the following brief review of all eight parts by describing the structure of the following sentence:

He smiled a happy smile and walked briskly to his office.

In this statement, the nouns are *smile* and *office* (things). The pronouns (words that stand in for persons and things) are *he* and *his.* The verbs indicating actions are *smiled* and *walked*. The adjective (a word describing a noun or pronoun) is *happy*. The adverb (a word describing verbs, adjectives or other adverbs) is *briskly*. The determiner (a word introducing a noun) is *a*. The preposition (a word that indicates a relationship between its object and something else in the sentence) is *to*, and the conjunction (a word that joins words, phrases or clauses) is *and*.

In terms of the above example, "Mama cooks" constitutes a sentence because it includes both a noun to serve as the subject of the sentence (Mama) and a verb (cooks) to serve as a predicate. In contrast, "Went fast" cannot stand as a sentence because there is no noun or pronoun to serve as the subject, only a verb (went) and an adverb (fast).[11] As might be evident from this brief example, teachers who don't understand nouns and verbs will have a difficult time alerting not only their English language learners but also fluent student speakers when they write a *sentence fragment* (a word group punctuated as a sentence but lacking a subject and predicate).

In terms of making messages comprehensible for English language learners, teachers can simplify English sentences without changing their key ideas by relying heavily on nouns, pronouns and verbs when they wish to communicate something to ELLs. Since the heart of the meaning in English sentences is typically found in subjects and verbs, the teacher might shape abbreviated messages to ELLs using only those words from a sentence. For example, in the statement "He smiled a happy smile and walked briskly to his office," the key words in terms of meaning are *he*, *smiled*, and *walked*. An ELL is likely to understand the words "He smiled...walked" more readily if they are not embedded in a much longer word string. Such adaption is easy to do (assuming the teacher can identify nouns, pronouns and verbs) and a great help to English language beginners. As ELLs develop more language skills, teachers can gradually lengthen messages by adding in more detail.

Such adaption of classroom discourse to the needs of individual English language learners falls into the category of *differentiated instruction.* Teachers are expected to make such adaption not only for ELLs, but for all students. Students in a classroom are never perfect replicas of each other; they all have individual strengths, weaknesses and needs. Teachers are expected to be able to identify what kind of instruction individual students need and to vary their instruction to provide it. For example, to address different levels of reading ability, the same information might be provided to students in very different formats. Suppose, for example, a class were learning about precipitation. Teachers might provide an illustration of rainfall, perhaps with a few key words, to ELLs; they might provide a passage explaining rainfall in simple words and sentences to struggling readers; and, they might provide a passage explaining rainfall that contains a variety of sentence structures as well as some new vocabulary words to more sophisticated readers. The ability to adapt messages in an effort to make them comprehensible for ELLs is just one part of the skill set teachers need as classroom professionals who must meet the needs of *all* students.

Word Order

English speakers arrange words serving different functions in a sentence in a particular order, and a change of word order affects its meaning. For example, consider the sentence "A dog bit my neighbor." If we change the word order, we can create the sentence "My neighbor bit a dog." These two sentences obviously have completely different meanings, with the first being common and the second being highly unlikely. Moreover, if we change the sentence to "bit my neighbor a dog," it becomes incomprehensible to English speakers. All of this is true because common word order in English is subject (dog)-verb (bit)-object (neighbor). And verb (bit)-subject (dog)-object (neighbor) is not acceptable. Other languages, however, use different patterns. For example, in Korean the word order is subject-object-verb, which in this example would produce the sentence "A dog my neighbor bit"—as well as Yonsu's sentence "Can I sticker put in here?" Teachers should be aware that ELLs often need explanations of appropriate word order in English.

Cognates

Cognates are words that have the same origin, or that mean the same thing in more than one language. For example, both English and French have the word *restaurant*, and it has the same meaning in both languages. Since Spanish and English have many cognates, they are an especially useful tool for vocabulary development in classrooms with many Spanish-speaking students. An online search can help teachers— and students—identify some of the most common and useful ones, including: *family/familia, insects/insectos, map/mapa, surprise/sorpresa,* and *activities/actividades. Borrowed words* or *loanwords* are words that one language has directly adopted from another, although pronunciation may well change because different languages incorporate a range of different sounds. For example, there are borrowed Korean words that equate to *television, truck* and other English words. These are another excellent way to build on first language knowledge that ELLs bring to the classroom. Teachers can replace key words with cognates and borrowed words to help English language learners understand the message of a sentence. Identifying such words in various languages is fairly easy, given the extensive resources online.

Morphemes

Morphemes are the smallest units of language that carry meaning. For example, in English, -*s* functions as a morpheme, because when it is added to a noun it changes the meaning from singular to plural (*boy/boys*, for example). In this case, the morpheme is also a suffix, or something added to the end of a word that changes meaning. *Un* in "unhappy" is also a morpheme, in this case falling into the category of a prefix, or something that is added to the beginning of a word that changes its meaning. Here, the *un* changes the meaning from "happy" to "not happy." Another morpheme is *–ed*, which changes a verb to past tense when it is added to a regular verb, as in *wait/waited.* Because morphemes are meaning-bearing language units, being familiar with them is enormously useful to ELLs as they work to expand their vocabulary. Teachers can make a list of common morphemes (including prefixes and suffixes) and explicitly teach them to English language learners; a list posted in the classroom would be a handy reference as well.

A word of caution: Our experience tells us that teachers would be wise to be exceedingly careful in teaching *–s* as a morpheme because it has more than one meaning in English and can easily be confusing for ELLs. As noted above, it typically indicates plurality for nouns. It also, however, appears as a marker for third person, singular verbs.[12] For example, we would say "They walk" (third person plural) but change the verb form in "She walks." Here, the *–s* is added to make the verb third person singular. The result is that while the *–s* suffix may look the same in different phrases, it may not have the same meaning. Consider, for example, "He eats a lot," and "His apples were delicious." Although *eats* and *apples* may look similar, the function of the *–s* is different for the verb ("eats") and the noun ("apples"). Here again is the argument for teachers having a good understanding of how English functions. Teachers themselves must be conscious of the fact that an *-s* at the end of a word has more than one meaning. Otherwise, not only will they have difficulty helping ELLs clear up their confusion—they may in fact be the cause of it.

Summary

It is critically important, first, that teachers always remember that language and power are inextricably intertwined and that no language or dialect is inherently superior to another. Instead, one language or dialect gains prominence and prestige because those who speak it are in a privileged position and wield power in and over the culture. The fact that some students don't speak English, or don't speak it fluently, indicates nothing about their ability to think or reason. They simply have one set of language skills rather than another. In addition, teachers should expect that it will take students some years after they develop conversational ability to master the academic discourse of the classroom.

Since communication is a two-way process, teachers have a responsibility to shape their messages to make them as comprehensible as possible to ELLs in their classroom, and to make a good faith effort to understand students' attempts to communicate in English. Having a good understanding of first and second language development as well as of key structural features of the English language will help teachers meet their responsibilities.

Explorations

1. Visit a local community where a language other than English is dominant, and write down messages on signs written in English. Then, analyze the signs to determine which elements of English the writers have mastered, which elements they don't yet seem to understand. Decide how the signs might be better worded—and what lesson you might offer to the sign's author. If, for example, words were out of order, how would you explain that?

2. Teachers have to be good diagnosticians to provide students with the right information at the right time, so practicing such analysis is important. Find some K-12 writing samples from someone who grew up speaking English and from an English language learner. It would be best to include your own writing if you can, and to have samples spanning some years. Look closely for patterns of growth as well as patterns of errors/confusion. Then, compare similarities and differences in each set of writing. Can you identify patterns for each writer related to the structures discussed above (lexical categories, cognates, word order, morphemes and such)? How is the development in the writing of the English language learner similar to or different from the writer whose first language is English?

3. Be adventurous! Go online and explore a particular language. See how much you can learn about features of that language that might be useful for teachers to know. Experiment with terms to use in your search—after all, that's what you'd likely have to do if you were in a school that had little support for classroom teachers of ELLs. Keep a list of particularly useful websites to share with your classmates.

Notes

1   This quotation has been attributed to both E. M. Forster and W. H. Auden—so we can't say with any certainty who actually said it.

2   Finnegan, E. (1994). *Language: Its structure and use* (2nd ed.). Orlando, FL: Harcourt Brace & Company.

3   We believe the work of Steven Pinker to be an exception and would encourage readers interested in language development to independently explore his work. See, for example, Pinker, S. (1994). *The language instinct.* New York: William Morrow.

4   Tomasello, M. (2003). *Constructing a language: A usage-based theory of language acquisition.* Cambridge, MA: Harvard University Press.

5   Lenneberg, E.H. (1969, May 9). On explaining language. *Science* (*164*) 3880, 635–643. doi: 10.2307/1725957

6   Brown, R. (1973). *A first language: The early stages.* Cambridge, MA: Harvard University Press.

7   Pinker, S. (1994). *The language instinct.* New York: William Morrow.

8   Hakuta, K. (1974). Prefabricated patterns and the emergence of structure in second language acquisition. *Language Learning*, *24*, 287–297. Retrieved from ERIC database. (ED 155 728).

9   Cummins, J. (1979). Cognitive/academic language proficiency, linguistic interdependence, the optimum age question and some other matters. *Working Papers on Bilingualism*, *19*, 121–129.

10 Hakuta, K., Butler, Y.G., & Witt, D. (2000). *How long does it take English learners to attain proficiency?* The University of California Linguistic Minority Research Institute Policy Report 2000-1. Retrieved September 12, 2012 from http://www.usc.edu/dept/education/CMMR/FullText/Hakuta_HOW_LONG_DOES_IT_TAKE.pdf

11 Those with a more advanced understanding of grammar may want to argue that they can imagine cases where *went fast* might actually serve as a sentence—but we're talking here about simple constructions, not more complex topics like implied subjects.

12 "Person" is a quality of nouns and pronouns. First person means the speaker/writer is included (*I*, *we*, *my* and so on); second person is *you* and *yours*; third person is everyone else (*girl*, *he*, *teacher*, *them* and so on).

CHAPTER FOUR

Nurturing Literacy in English

How Does This Magic Happen?

Most English-speaking Americans are literate; that is, they can read and write. And, though few people think much about it, Americans use literacy every day for a wide range of purposes. They read books for advice on how to manage their time and money. They read manuals to figure out how to install a computer program. They write e-mails asking their colleagues for information, complaining to their friends about their significant others, and reporting progress to their bosses. When we look carefully at what people do with literacy, however, we realize that it is much more than the ability to write b-r-e-a-d on a grocery list or to read o-p-e-n on the door of a repair shop.

Literacy is a tool for making things happen in the world. Indeed, it is a tool for changing the world itself. Recent events offer a useful illustration. A wave of major protests across the Arab world that began in late 2010, commonly known as the Arab Spring, forced new leadership in Tunisia, Egypt, Libya and Yemen; civil unrest continues in several other countries in the region. These events depended heavily on social media, which has opened new possibilities for communication in repressive societies. In this case, it allowed citizens to share information with each other and the world, as well as to plan concerted political actions. Still: the existence of social media itself would be meaningless if citizens couldn't read and write. It was essentially literacy that enabled these citizens to substantively change the shape of their societies. What power is greater?

It seems like magic: People learn to associate certain squiggles on a piece of paper or a computer screen with certain meanings...and then they can change the world. How does this magic happen? As the word *magic* suggests, much happens offstage—out of our conscious awareness.

In this chapter we explore that offstage world and its relevance to teachers, students and classrooms by exploring three key questions:

What is literacy? How does literacy in English develop? And, what are the social consequences of English language learners developing—or not developing—literacy in English? The answers to those questions obviously have enormous implications for classrooms, which we'll discuss along the way.

What Is Literacy?

Definitions: Who Cares? (You Should!)

You may consider us boring professors because we want to start with definitions. OK: guilty as charged. But give us a moment to show you why definition is an essential first step.

In the early 20th century, an interesting guy (that is, a famous philosopher) named Ludwig Wittgenstein pointed out that everyday language is problematic because one word—say, *leaf*—can be understood very differently by different people.[1] In our classes we demonstrate the validity of that point by asking students to draw a leaf. Recently, in a class of 19 students, no two leaves remotely resembled each other. This is true, as Wittgenstein suggests, because the pictures in our mind that a word conjures up depend on our experiences in the real world. People familiar with oak trees try to draw oak leaves; people familiar with poplar trees try to draw poplar leaves, and so on. Consider what's happening here: a teacher asks if everyone knows what a *leaf* is and looks like, and everyone answers yes—but the definition and picture in each person's head is different. Hmmm. Quite a lot of confusion could arise later from such an unstable foundation.

Words matter, and making sure everyone understands the same word in the same way is essential to effective communication. So: before we go on discuss how literacy develops, let's be sure we all have the same understanding of what literacy *is*—which, as it happens, will require some other definitions along the way. Bear with us.

The World as Text, Reading as Transaction, and Emergent Literacy

If literacy involves people *reading texts*, then we'd better be clear about what we mean by *texts* and *reading*.

The World as Text. In his book *World on Paper*,[2] David Olson argued that literacy is more than reading and writing. It is, he argued, humans' ability to manipulate a wide variety of resources for a range of purposes. To make his case, he traced literacy artifacts throughout human history and analyzed the functions of literacy. Typically, we think of writing as the way people record their thoughts, but Olson also looked at other ways people have communicated their thinking, such as paintings and stained glass windows in cathedrals—which he termed *literacy artifacts.* At a time when relatively few people had learned to read and write, such artifacts served as alternative communication systems, ways to convey messages to the public about important topics like nature and divinity. Throughout history, humans have used a variety of communication systems, not just written language, to send messages and/or influence events. This means, of course, that people potentially have *multiple literacies*—or, the ability to send and make sense of messages in a wide variety of formats. Written language is certainly one means of communication—but only one.

We speak, for example, of *computer literacy* as the ability to use computers and other digital media. Computers have extended the possibilities of communication (with, for example, the ability to create hypertext), just as writing moved possibilities beyond drawing. Or, many schools now offer courses in *media literacy*, which help people understand how text, photos and videos can all be manipulated to create a particular effect on the audience. Print ads, for example, use pictures, words and graphics to try to persuade people to buy something, whereas movies often try to evoke particular emotions through selected sights and sounds.

We believe people use multiple literacies—that is, they have the ability to craft and comprehend messages using a variety of means of communication. From this perspective the ability to *read* a *text* includes being able to make sense of materials ranging from a YouTube video to a Shakespearean sonnet. For this reason, contemporary teachers who embrace this perspective—as we do—often talk about teaching their students to *read the world*, not just books and other print texts.[3]

We hasten to add that this perspective does not discount the importance of being able to read and compose in print text, of course, because written language does offer some distinct advantages. For example, Olson worked extensively with young children and noted that before they learn to read and write, they indicate their concept of number by drawing the same symbol over and over to indicate *more-than-one*—the same meaning captured in writing by the morpheme –s. Olson notes that in this regard, children's behavior reflects human history. It took some time for humans to understand that they could use a symbol to represent *more-than-one*, and they too used several drawings of the same thing to indicate multiplicity. Surely both the child telling about her family by drawing its six cats and the cave artist telling about a hunt by drawing ten bears would agree with equal enthusiasm that written language and the modest morpheme –s is an incredibly useful, time-saving tool. How much easier to write *six cats* or *ten bears* than to draw them!

Having noted our appreciation for print, we'll return to the point we made above: There are many varieties of *literacy* and many things we consider *texts*. Keep that in mind, because it has substantive implications for the classroom, which we'll discuss later. But first, since we're going to be talking more about ELLs' ability to read and write in English, we need to shore up the foundation we're building here by defining still two more terms. The first is *reading as transaction* and the second is *emergent literacy*.

Reading as Transaction. Most people do understand that reading is a process and that words don't leap instantaneously from page to brain. For example, most students have spent time puzzling over a passage in a textbook, just as most adults have spent time puzzling over "simple" instructions for operating a new gadget. Most people also understand that *learning* to read is a process; the child who can recognize the letter *b* does not necessarily recognize the word *bed*. However, some assumptions that people have made over time about *reading* have, like the idea that written texts are the only things people *read*, been challenged by recent research.

For example, many people thought (and some still do think) that reading is primarily a decoding activity—that meaning resides *in* the words and that if we simply teach children the sounds of letters and the spelling of familiar words (with some vocabulary tossed in), they will have learned *to read.* From this perspective, if a child is reading a text aloud and correctly pronounces a word on the page as *habitat*, then the child has correctly read the text. But as Wittgenstein demonstrated, meaning does not reside only in words themselves. Instead, the words people use always reflect some meaning in their heads, which may or may not agree with the meanings in other people's heads.

Interestingly, from this perspective (which is our perspective), the child who said not *habitat* but *home* in the above example would be correct because the meaning of *home* appears to neatly match the mental model most people have of *habitat*. That is, the child did a good job of making sense of the word on the page. The classroom implications here are obvious: how a teacher defines reading will govern whether a child is corrected—or praised—for saying *home* when the literal word that appeared on the page was *habitat*. While some people cling to the idea that decoding equates to reading, others (like us) insist that reading involves readers making personal sense of a text. In fact, we would say that a child who pronounced *habitat* correctly upon seeing it in print but who had no idea what it meant had not *read* the word.

In short, we accept the definition of *reading* famously articulated by Louise Rosenblatt, which incorporates the role of the reader's experience in determining meaning.[4] She defined reading as a *transaction* between a reader and a text in which readers draw not only on the printed page (*habitat*) but also on their own experience to develop a personal understanding of a text (*home*). Meaning lies not exclusively in the words (or else students wouldn't draw different leaves), nor in the reader (because no student could reasonably draw a large animal with a trunk and call it a *leaf*). Instead, as they interact with the text, readers create meaning that is in some way unique to each of them.

This is so because many factors in their experience (like which leaves they may or may not have ever seen) affect the meaning they derive from the words. When we refer to *reading process*, then, we are referring to the process as Rosenblatt explained it: a transaction between reader and text that generates an understanding that is unavoidably unique to the reader in some way.[5] Of course students learn skills (like phonics) along the way; after they have the experience of a Dr. Seuss book, for example, their experience is likely to inform them that the letters *at* have the same sound in several words, like *cat* and *hat*. But the emphasis is on making meaning, drawing on what readers know from their life experience to make sense of the print words on a page.

Emergent Literacy. Just as there are different interpretations of what it means to read, there are different interpretations of when and how children begin to learn to read and write. When reading was thought to be a process of extracting meaning inherent in the words on the page, literacy was considered largely a matter of being able to discriminate among different letters and words. In order to learn to discriminate among the squiggles we call letters, people assumed that children had to have some other abilities in place first—for example, the ability to stay within the lines while coloring or to match shapes like circles. Some schools—especially private schools—tested young children to see if they had developed such skills before allowing them into classes explicitly teaching reading and writing. Without such skills, people thought, children wouldn't be ready for instruction and couldn't benefit from it.

As we've already noted, however, many scholars now accept a more complex definition of literacy, and with it has come some new understandings about what helps children learn to read and write. An important contributor to new thinking was Emilia Ferreiro,[6] an Argentinean scholar who studied how young children of various social backgrounds come to know the nature and function of writing systems. Her research demonstrated that social environment plays a significant role in children's literacy learning.

For example, we know that if children see adults in their home routinely reading newspapers and books, they arrive at school understanding some things about the purposes of reading and the forms of texts. Now, rather than thinking of reading as a linear process with some fixed point at which children are "ready" to learn to read and write, we embrace the concept of *emergent literacy*, of literacy as something that develops over time as children encounter a variety of environments that increase their understanding of what reading and writing are and what purposes they serve. An important educational implication of Ferreiro's research is that excluding children from schools because they haven't already learned some things at home limits their opportunities to learn and further delays their progress.

This is important, because in some places the old standards for *reading* readiness, like recognizing circles, have been replaced by new ones, like having had experience with adults reading them books or being familiar with the alphabet. We know now that literacy begins with a host of experiences that can take place either in the home or in schools—and that for children who haven't had experience with the world of print at home, exposure at school (or in such programs as Head Start) needs to be provided as early as possible.

Finally: A Definition of Literacy

Given the influence of the theorists we've cited above, we believe *literacy* is the ability to use a variety of message systems, including language, to make things happen in the world. Language systems are particularly useful and flexible tools, since they serve equally well to record our thoughts—or to help overthrow a dictator. While the discussion below focuses on *literacy in the English language*, it is important for readers to remember that being unable to read and write in English is not the same thing as being illiterate, and that print texts are just one of many texts people can learn to read. We *read* not only words on the page, but the entire world around us—just as we compose using not only words but images and sounds.

Implications: Literacy as Power in the World

There is a great deal of rather meaningless language around literacy, pretty much amounting to "Of course everyone needs to learn to read and write." Why exactly print literacy is so critical, however, is rarely thought about, let alone talked about. Nor do we talk much about different types of literacy or their relative value based on social norms. These are important issues, however, and to explore them a bit we want to stop here and ask you to think back to earlier parts of this text. Remember: cultural norms are often invisible, and every culture is chock full of ingroups and outgroups. In U.S. society, one ingroup/outgroup distinction is made when some people are considered literate (and therefore smart and valuable) others not, or not-so, literate (and therefore stupid and not valuable). Think about how these definitions function in relation to power.

For example, consider whose writing is read, whose voice is heard in the public arena. If we consider the magazines and books that are written, the speeches that are made, the people who are interviewed and quoted, it becomes clear that cultural credibility is given almost exclusively to highly educated or highly positioned people whose speech and writing conforms to a very narrow standard (the hypothetical standardized English discussed earlier). Bankers and politicians debate fiscal policy, while professors and politicians debate educational policy. These people clearly qualify as literate, based on cultural norms.

However, a much wider range of citizens than those who speak and write in newscaster English may have useful knowledge to contribute to policy deliberations. A politician may say "This policy is sure to relieve the suffering of our hard working farmers," but it's possible that the politician knows less about the likely impact of the proposed policy on real people than the farmer just in from the fields who listens and says to himself "This ain't gonna help me none." Polite society would likely, however, dismiss the farmer as unintelligent (not-so-literate), based on the particular way he constructed his sentence—that is, on his dialect. Think, too, about different kinds of texts, different varieties of literacy. For an example closer to the classroom, consider these questions: Who is more literate about his community—the teacher who grimaces at graffiti on his city's walls, or the child who can readily make sense of that urban communication system? Who might be more literate about ways to cut daily expenses—the teacher who grew up in a comfortable middle class family, or the high school senior who is head of his household, working to help support the family while concurrently managing its finances and trying to graduate?

Of course politicians and teachers and other people who speak newscaster English know things—but our point here is that they are not the only ones who have valuable knowledge. When other voices are ignored, or their particular dialect is considered a mark of stupidity (as Amy Tan perceived her mother's dialect), then the valuable insights they may have are lost and decisions are less well-informed.

There are several advantages to be gained if more credibility were extended to a wider range of voices than is now the case—if the ideas in writing could be taken seriously even before the writers had mastered a semicolon. It is ironic that although teachers complain about politicians making policy for classrooms without ever having taught a class, they are among the many people who do not take seriously the experiences and thinking of students and parents whose abilities with spoken and written language they deem less sophisticated than their own. In speaking and writing about their experiences, ELLs and their parents offer a window into areas where *they* are the experts, and even if their subjects and verbs don't agree, they can provide as much instruction to the teacher about their culture and community as the teacher can provide to the students about reading, writing and arithmetic.

What does this all mean? In the simplest of terms, it means that we believe teachers should be among the first to recognize that marginalized voices and perspectives—including those of ELLs and their parents—often have much to offer to those who take time to listen and try to understand. Teachers have much to share with students about the English language, but students and their parents have much to share with teachers about their perspectives and experiences. More on that to come below.

How Does Literacy in English Develop?

Having just called attention to the ways in which many voices are misunderstood and marginalized, we begin our exploration of how people learn to read and write in English with some thinking about how schools contribute to such marginalization.

Teachers' Misreading

In school lounges, it's common to hear a teacher remark that a particular child lacks literacy skills because his or her family doesn't have books at home and doesn't value reading and writing. Unfortunately, teachers often rush to such conclusions based only on their own backgrounds and experience. For example, one of us once participated in a meeting with teachers from a local school. Asked which language-minority group in the community would need help from university faculty, a few teachers immediately pointed to families affiliated with a particular church. The teachers believed that the families had only Bibles in their homes, and they understood that to mean that the families did not value literacy generally. However, a visit to the church revealed that although it did not have typical Sunday school classes (and readers and workbooks), it did have many books that its members might read, and many reading and writing activities (like expressing their faith in poetry) in which members participated.

Teachers unfamiliar with forms of literacy outside their own experience are often unaware of the difference between school-based and community-based activities. Being unfamiliar with them, teachers simply assume they don't exist. As a result, students often receive poor assessments from their teachers—not because they lack ability, but because the teachers simply don't understand the particular ways that literacy practices in their home communities have shaped their performance.

A stunning example comes from the work of Shirley Brice Heath.[7] She detailed two communities that engaged in literacy activities meaningful to them, but which differed not only from each other but also from typical classroom activities. One community was highly religious. In that community, the word *story* meant a truthful account of something that really happened, usually intended to teach listeners a lesson. In the other community, storytelling was a highly prized community activity in which a *story* might have begun in some kernel of truth, but which the teller embellished with great exaggeration and word play. In this second community, the standard for storytelling was not truthfulness, or moral, or even plot; its purpose was strictly to entertain, and the more outlandish the story, the better it was received.

Children in both schools were failing, and eventually Heath was able to convincingly explain why. Asked to explain the students' shortcomings, teachers in the first community (whose definition of *story* hinged upon the many children's books they'd read about princesses and such) judged the children so dull they couldn't even invent a story on their own. Meanwhile, teachers in the second community found the children scattered and illogical (not to mention being flat out liars), unable to put together a story with a beginning, middle and end. Based on the norms of their community, children in both schools knew perfectly well what a *story* was and could perform one on demand. It was only when the teachers' definition of *story* was completely different that the children were made to seem inept. (There's that *leaf* problem again!)

In working with ELLs, it's only natural that teachers would have in mind their own experiences teaching reading and writing to children who have spoken English since birth. However, ELLs have very different life experiences with language and culture, and if teachers don't stop to consider differences, their assumptions may derail their instructional efforts. Something to keep in mind: if teachers don't see students meeting expectations, it's a better idea to check for differences in children's experiential background than to immediately decide that the children lack ability. With that in mind, we next explore some differences in literacy acquisition for ELLs.

Literacy in First Language vs. Second Language

Literacy development in the first language builds upon oral language that children develop from birth. Research on English-speaking children's invented spelling, for example, has demonstrated that the invented spelling typical of very young writers reflects an emerging knowledge of sound-letter relationships. The work of Glenda Bissex,[8] who studied her son Paul's development, offers a wealth of examples, including the title of her book on the subject: *Gnys at Wrk*. While Paul didn't get it exactly right, we can see that he got the *G* and *n* right for *genius*, as well as a reasonable try of the *ys* sound for *ius*. In *Wrk*, he missed only the *o*.

Bissex's work also produced other insights. She found that Paul's reading and writing skills developed at a similar pace, for example, and he began building both based on his oral language skills. In addition, Paul's growth suggested that exposure to environmental print is important for reading development. When children view signs reading *IN* or *OUT*, for example, they notice letters and so begin learning about alphabetic principles. Overall, what Bissex and other researchers have demonstrated is that children can and do take substantive steps toward literacy in their first language on their own, in part because they are in the habit of trying to make sense of their experiences. Just as babies work independently to make sense of the stream of oral language flowing around them, children often work independently to make sense of the world of print.

However, as Paul began schooling, his independent discoveries about reading and writing were replaced by teacher-initiated school literacy activities. Other research also suggests that once children begin school, school literacy activities rather than their own initiative drive their literacy development. School literacy activities build on students' oral language and assumed life experiences, including assumptions about exposure to print and certain kinds of texts, like typical children's storybooks. With the shift to school-based experiences, children who learned English from birth seem to share a similar path to literacy. Table 1 offers a snapshot of a typical progression, one reported by our students based on writing samples from their own K-12 education.

Table 1. Pre-service Teachers' Analysis of Their Own Writing Samples

Grades	Topics & Interests	Experiences	Knowledge	Genre
0–preschool	Super heroes Toys Family Holidays All about me	Sheltered home experiences Fairy tales Stories Family TV watching & TV stories Holidays	Minimal real life experiences, activities & structure Knowledge of the world in which we function Our own name (the only thing we were certainly able to spell) Letters (mixed capital and lower case)	Made-up stories & fairy tales Illustrations and writing about a picture Drawings Recounts of experiences Penmanship & tracing letters
K–3	Family Developing personal interests and friendship Animals Drawings Basic storytelling and creativity Holidays Math word problems (e.g., subtraction)	Family, relationships (friends but still naïve) & social events Personal experiences Sports & school activities School writing School assignments Pop culture (e.g., Nintendo)	Quantity (more & less), addition, & subtraction Transitional spelling knowledge (a mix of phonemic and letter-name spelling such as atomick, serender) Capitalization & punctuation Developed sentences and more description with fewer spelling errors Evaluate own writing	Short poems Journals Stories Likes & dislikes Science fiction

Continued

Table 1. Pre-service Teachers' Analysis of Their Own Writing Samples (continued)

Grades	Topics & Interests	Experiences	Knowledge	Genre
4–6 Middle school	Sports Friends More school and social life (less home life) Many hobbies School projects Play dates with friends Girl sleepovers Drugs & alcohol	Emerging under-standing of social norms and groups (e.g., clicks) Self-discovery of social groups and stereotypes Research School projects Friend parties	Proper grammar and sentence structure (noun, verb, more de-scriptive and longer sentences) Spelling errors are careless not lack of knowledge Compare & contrast Format of re-search papers (science, envi-ronment) Poetry (color, free verse, representa-tion) Literature, histori-cal events, society, religion, and world cultures	Journals Book reports Short essays Research projects Persuasive essays Narrative Autobiography
High school	Personal issues Self-discovery Identity analysis Grade-oriented writing (school, assignments such as writing with prompt, books, history) Future-oriented School History Friends outside school Literary devices	Friends are most important Personal interests & passions Freedom, love personal analysis Sports & practices Religion & religious retreat Becoming more independent Introduction to col-lege preparation Self-discovery Art School assignment	Understand com-plex sentence structure and writing with a thesis Metaphor & per-sonification	Analytic essays Detailed poetry Complex writing Personal narra-tives Lengthy papers Book reviews Critical analysis Short answer worksheet (defini-tion), Document-based Questions (DBQs)

As the table suggests, English-speaking students develop literacy skills in schools through a predictable progression of reading and writing activities that move from a focus on self, to family and friends, to issues in the larger society. The nature of writing becomes steadily more analytical and more oriented toward real world tasks. Writing samples also show a progression in students' understanding of English conventions and spelling, moving for example from invented spelling (which nevertheless can often be understood by a patient adult) to conventional spelling. In short, research in the United States and other English-speaking countries indicates that when English is the first language, literacy development builds upon oral language skills that young children develop from birth. And, it moves through a predictable sequence that corresponds to typical school literacy curricula. Such is not the case for ELLs, however.

A variety of factors influence the development of English literacy for individual ELLs. One is the time at which the student enters school in an English-speaking country. Young children born in homes in the U.S. where parents speak home languages other than English generally follow the same path that English speakers take.[9] Students who arrive in the upper elementary grades and above, however, have extremely diverse development patterns because there are so many variables that affect their progress. One of the most important challenges that this age group faces is that they must learn to read in English at the same time that they are reading to learn academic content—a double challenge. Moreover, texts become more complex and difficult to comprehend as they move to higher grade levels.

Although many ELLs developed cognitive skills as they learned to read and write in their native languages, and although their first language does provide them with language resources, the literacy skills of the first language are not directly transferrable to reading, writing and functioning in English. For example, learning that the object is placed in front of a verb in a first language may lead to errors in English, as we've already discussed. Then, too, as we also discussed earlier, the fact that identity is intertwined with language further affects development of literacy in English, especially for older students.[10]

What seems unique about English language learners is that they often develop English literacy skills *before* they demonstrate ability with oral language. That is, they may understand a good bit of written English before they can speak spontaneously. At the same time, their decoding skills do not necessarily match the level of their text comprehension. Some English language learners master phonics and demonstrate excellent decoding skills—but they may not be able to say what the words they can pronounce actually mean (like a child who can say, but not define, *habitat*).

Interestingly, despite the fact that skills from the first language don't translate directly to skills in English, literacy experiences in the first language do offer students valuable resources to draw on (even if they sometimes lead students astray). For example, students who experienced textbooks in their first language know something about the purpose and content of textbooks that can help them approach a textbook in English. Or, an understanding of writing in their first language may allow them to use it to support their efforts in English. For example, Yonsu, an 8-year-old from Korea, used Korean orthography to help her identify her weekly spelling word list, translating the heading into Korean to remember what the list was and was for (see Figure 1). Literacy in a first language, then, is extremely helpful in cultivating literacy in a second language, even if it's true that what students know about their first language can lead them astray at times in English.

Figure 1. Yonsu's use of first language literacy to support second language literacy

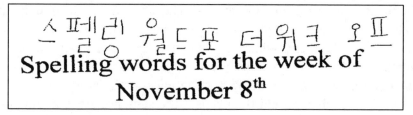

Oral Language Development

Many readers may recall experiences in their high school language classes that can illuminate what we said above: that English language learners who arrive in U.S. schools after grades preK–1 typically read and write in English before they develop skill in speaking it. More specifically, we believe that many readers whose first language is English may remember being able to read orally from their high school Spanish or French textbooks. Yet, even if they were able to read words like *mesa* or *vous* reasonably well aloud, they may also remember praying that the teacher would never call on them to generate an original spoken sentence. Reading some foreign words on a page is one thing; calling to mind a bunch of foreign words and stringing them together in a new pattern is quite another. It's hardly surprising that in second language learning, the ability to read often comes before the ability to generate original oral sentences.

Learners working to develop literacy in a first language depend heavily on their knowledge of oral language, but the situation tends to be reversed for second language learning. That is, learners who already know how to read and write in one language can draw on what they know about reading and writing to develop literacy in a second language. For ELLs, literacy in English offers useful support learning to speak it. For example, if a teacher were to ask a student where the classroom dictionary was, being able to read the printed word *table* on a word wall in the classroom would be a great help to the student trying to respond orally.

There are two important implications for teachers here. The first is that teachers should not be alarmed if ELLs initially speak as little as possible. Early silence or hesitation to speak are not reliable indicators of whether or not a student has learned anything about English, but instead are typical of the second language learning process. After all, many teachers would likely have behaved the same way in their own high school and college language classes. The second implication is that teachers should be especially conscious of providing support for oral language development, which may be the most challenging aspect of learning English for many ELLs. For example, a teacher might help a student respond orally by modeling a sentence stem, as in *I like xxx because....* The student would then repeat the sentence stem, adding only the missing information about his or her own preferences, rather than having to generate an entirely new response. Providing such support, commonly called *scaffolding*, can help ELLs practice oral language without being overwhelmed.

Implications: Cultural Capital and Classroom Discourse

The ideas we've been detailing—about multiple literacies and texts, about limited perceptions of who is and is not literate, and about cultural assumptions coloring the perspective of teachers in unfortunate ways—all have enormous implications for the classroom. We began sketching some of those above when we argued that more attention needs to be paid to marginalized voices because people who speak newscaster English are not the only people in the world with valuable knowledge. Here, we look more closely at that idea and at how marginalizing minority voices derails the education of English language learners.

Cultural Capital. A philosophical concept useful in explaining how people become marginalized in the first place is that known as *cultural capital,* a term coined by the French sociologist Bourdieu.[11] It refers to the knowledge that one class of people has that another doesn't because of their different life experiences. For example, some people will recognize the acronym *NPR* (National Public Radio) immediately while others won't because its listeners tend to be relatively privileged. On the way to reaching his conclusion, Bourdieu compared family activities in more and less privileged homes and demonstrated that school activities most closely resemble home activities of families with more resources, like visiting museums, attending classical concerts, and so on. In other words, some families can provide their children with life experiences that give them an advantage over other children in schools. Conversely, children who don't come to school with certain types of mainstream experiences are at a disadvantage, often reflected in their teachers judging them to be less smart or less able than their mainstream peers. Perhaps the most obvious example of this is the teacher who is secretly (or not) critical of a family because the adults never read to their children, no matter how many other things the parents may have taught the children about their culture, history, values and other important topics.

The assumption that some kinds of knowledge are more valuable than others also means that the kinds of texts that enter mainstream classrooms are very limited. For example, most students in U.S. schools must read poetry by Robert Frost and John Keats, even if they have never seen snow or a Grecian urn. Despite the difficulty children have connecting such poems and other canonical literature to their life experience, such artifacts are what fill the classroom. It might be otherwise. A world of texts that students might connect with more readily exists and could be used to enrich students' in-school literacy activities.

For example, popular music frequently makes serious charges about social inequities, like sexism and racism. *Huckleberry Finn* can remain in the classroom (it is a pretty darned entertaining book, after all), but teachers might also bring in some related popular music dealing with racism. *Guernica* is protest art, and well worth being familiar with; teachers might prompt students to think more deeply by asking them to consider whether or not it's possible for graffiti to serve as protest art for some urban populations. (Graffiti has, after all, been in use since the Greeks and Romans.) Providing such opportunities promotes *intertextuality*—the ability to use one text to deepen the understanding of another. Understanding becomes layered, and richer, when various literacy artifacts are allowed to bump into each other in a classroom, jarring students into deeper thinking about important issues and new awareness of human interconnectedness in the world.

But, when the parameters of valuable knowledge are limited in the ways common to classrooms, many young people are effectively told that their experiences as captured in their music, words and art are not valuable—and neither, it is implied, are they. This is the reality for all American students with limited family means, and it is magnified for ELLs. Their language is devalued. Their home life is devalued. Their community life is devalued. Their cultural art and music and heroes and holidays are devalued. Rather than trying to learn what they know and build on it, too often teachers consider them empty vessels containing no worthwhile knowledge or experience. Is it any wonder, then, that so many Latinos and other ELLs give up or drop out when the environment they find themselves in finds nothing valuable in their identities?

Every student comes to the classroom with experiences and perspectives that can contribute to his or her learning. We urge teachers to avoid falling into the habit of dismissing students whose life experiences are *different*, not lesser, and to find ways to build on those experiences by becoming familiar with and explicitly valuing them. To do otherwise is not only to devalue the students that schools profess to help, but to squander the potential for learning they bring with them.

Classroom Discourse. An important part of learning English is, of course, learning how to speak it. Classroom discourse tends to follow a particular pattern, and the way teachers apply the pattern to ELLs contributes to the devaluing problem discussed above. Typically, teachers initiate a question (I) and students, often chosen by the teachers, respond (R), and then teachers evaluate the appropriateness of the student response (E). This IRE sequence limits the range of responses students can give and again limits opportunities for students to bring their home experiences into the classroom. Courtney Cazden captured the way this pattern can work to disadvantage ELLs.[12] She found that teachers often ask students from mainstream backgrounds high-level comprehension questions, while they ask students from minority backgrounds low-level recall questions. Moreover, minority students often know the difference and feel as though their teachers are short-changing them and treating them as if they are not smart. Such patterns of teacher behavior are generally unconscious, a result of teachers absorbing and privileging their own cultural norms without being aware of it. They may not be aware of the harm they do, but it exists nevertheless.

To change classroom talk and build continuity between home and school experiences, all students—including English language learners—need to have opportunities to initiate classroom discourse, to take a turn participating in classroom discourse, and to evaluate their own responses after they receive formative feedback from the teacher. Some examples are found in the work of Kathryn Au, who studied how making a place for students' home experiences can support the learning of minority children in the classroom.[13] In Hawaii, where students of Hawaiian heritage are considered a minority population, she found that teachers successfully used Hawaiian talk story, the language of many students' homes, to engage the students meaningfully in literacy activities and to improve their reading comprehension. Au also found that teachers who come from students' cultural and socio-economic backgrounds persist in using effective instructional strategies they learned in teacher education programs, perhaps because they better understand the home/school disjuncture. Overall, she demonstrated that teachers can restructure their classroom learning environments in ways that support language-minority students' success and allow them to develop literacy along with their mainstream classmates. To do so, however, teachers need knowledge of students' home lives, which they may need to actively cultivate if their background differs from their students'.

Literacy: Beyond C-A-T and into Social Consequences

We began in Chapter One by detailing the achievement gap for English language learners, which is due at least in part to the fact that so many of them have limited literacy in the English language. If they cannot comprehend their textbooks, and if they cannot complete assigned written work in a form comprehensible to their teachers, their grades and learning both suffer. As we said above, it is no surprise that they often give up and drop out. For the individual student and his or her family, this outcome means a limited future, a limited ability to contribute to the family's means and stability. We want here, however, to point out that there are consequences to school failure that go beyond the individual and family.

The impact of literacy at a societal level is evident in the correlation of delinquency and illiteracy. A high percentage of incarcerated youth have low literacy skills, and a high percentage of incarcerated youth are only at the beginning of a lifetime of repeated incarceration. However, youths who develop reading skills return to state prison systems time after time at a lower rate. A study conducted by Criminal Justice Policy Council suggests "young, uneducated prisoners were 37% less likely to return to prison if they learned to read while incarcerated"(Keith & Mccray, 2002, p. 697).[14] In fact, the effect is great enough that states are increasing their efforts to provide alternative education for incarcerated youths. If literacy has a great enough impact for prison personnel and politicians to take note, shouldn't schools—and teachers—be redoubling their efforts to help students develop skills essential to their future? Surely the country would benefit from more effective literacy instruction for ELLs, a step toward reducing the 44% of adult English language learners who, according to the 2003 National Assessment of Adult Literacy, lack even the most basic literacy skills.

And here's one more thought. As many economists pointed out, 21st century jobs require advanced literacy skills and often a college education. We also know that ELLs will constitute a steadily increasing percentage of the U.S. work force—and it is people who are well established in the work force who are now positioned to realize the dream of buying a home. In weakening a growing percentage of the work force, we may also be weakening the future market for home sales, a major factor in the recession being experienced early in the 21st century.

In short, the cost of failing ELLs in schools is high. And, it has potential ramifications for everyone.

Summary

Literacy is a way to make things happen in the world. Print literacy and conventional texts are important, but many other literacies and texts exist that might enrich the typical classroom. Literacy is built upon student experience with language and the world, but there is often a disconnect between ELLs' life experiences and classroom expectations. Because school and society severely limit what knowledge is considered valuable, students from non-mainstream communities are often disadvantaged. When they fail, harmful consequences can accrue not only to individuals and their families, but to society at large. However, teachers who consciously strategize to help ELLs and other disadvantaged students succeed in developing literacy can create meaningful change in their classrooms, in students' lives, and in tomorrow's society.

Explorations

1. Although we rarely realize it, our values are reflected in the topics we choose to discuss and the kinds of stories we tell about ourselves. Consider the conversations your family may have over dinner or during family get-togethers. Try to capture common words, phrases and topics that reveal how family membership shapes our perspective on the world.

2. Read Elizabeth Bishop's poem "One Art," and find a popular song lyric that relates to its theme of loss. Be prepared to discuss with your classmates similarities and differences in the two works, thinking about how each piece is valued differently by peers, teachers and family members.

3. When you have a chance to visit K–12 classrooms, record teachers' questions. What types of questions do teachers ask, and what do students say in response? Can you identify patterns? In what way do students reveal their understanding, or lack of understanding, of classroom discourse? (You might consider the kinds of things students *don't* say as well as what they do.)

4. Take a look at the Common Core standards for language arts, which are being implemented across the U.S. Identify concepts and skills for the grade levels of your choice, and examine some textbooks to review the kinds of texts being used to teach them. What types of materials are

common? For at least one type of text, provide an example of a different type of text that might also be brought into the classroom.

Notes

1　Wittgenstein, L. (1968). *Philosophical investigations* (3rd. ed.). New York: Macmillan Publishing Co., Inc.

2　Olson, D.R. (1994). *The world on paper: The conceptual and cognitive implications of writing and reading.* Cambridge, UK: Cambridge University Press.

3　Freire, P., & Macedo, D. (1987). *Literacy: Reading the word and the world.* New York: Routledge. For a demonstration of what this idea means for the classroom, see, for example, Hinchey, P.H. (2001, May). Learning to read the world: Who—and what— is missing? *Reading Online, 4*(10). Retrieved from http://www.readingonline.org/ newliteracies/lit_index.asp?HREF=/newliteracies/hinchey/index.html

4　Rosenblatt, L.M. (1978). *The reader, the text, the poem: Transactional theory of the literacy work.* Carbondale, IL: Southern Illinois University Press.

5　In anticipation of protests that endorsing a transactional definition of reading means that "anything goes," we explicitly reject that inference here. As we've already noted, readers cannot assign any meaning they choose to any word at all. Defensible readings of a text are anchored in the actual words that appear there. We are simply admitting the possibility that one text may mean different things to different people. For example, some people might interpret a bumper sticker like "Bring the troops home" as advocating a sensible reaction to an unreasonable military action, while other readers would interpret it as a cowardly suggestion indicating lack of commitment to government policy. Here, there is no dispute about the words, but different meanings are assigned based on the political sensibilities of the readers. Moreover, no reader could defend an interpretation suggesting "It means dessert was good last night."

6　Goodman, Y., Reyes, I., & McArthur, K. (2005). Emilia Ferreiro: Searching for children's understanding about literacy as a cultural object. *Language Arts, 2*(4), 318–322.

7　Heath, S. B. (1983). *Ways with words: Language, life, and work in communities and classrooms.* Cambridge, UK: Cambridge University Press.

8　Bissex, G. L. (1980), *Gnys at wrk: A child learns to write and read.* Cambridge, MA: Harvard University Press.

9　Fitzgerald, J., & Noblit, G. W. (1999, June). About hopes, aspirations, and uncertainty: First-grade English-language learners' emergent reading. *Journal of Literacy Research, 31*(2), 133–182.

10　Valdés, G. (2001). *Learning and not learning English: Latino students in American schools.* New York: Teachers College Press.

11　Bourdieu, P. (1977). Cultural reproduction and social reproduction. In J. Karable & A.H. Halsey (Eds.), *Power and ideology in education* (pp. 487–511). New York: Oxford University Press.

12   Cazden, C.B. (1988). *Classroom discourse: The language of teaching and learning.* Portsmouth, NH: Heinemann.

13   Au, K.H. (2000). Literacy education in the process of community development. In T. Shanahan & F.V. Rodriguez-Brown (Eds.), *49th Yearbook of the National Reading Conference* (pp. 61–77). Chicago: National Reading Conference.

14   Keith, J. M. & Mccray, J. M. (2002). Juvenile offenders with special needs: Critical issues and bleak outcomes. *Journal of Qualitative Studies in Education, 15*(6), 691–710. doi:10.1080/0951839022000014385

CHAPTER FIVE

Effective Instruction and Assessment

Good Teaching for ELLs Is Good Teaching

If there is one thing we have learned from working with aspiring teachers, it is that they are impatient with theory and ever anxious to learn *how* to work effectively in classrooms. "Just tell me what to do," they often plead, most often because they fear falling short of their own ideals. That is, they fear being in a classroom and finding themselves inadequately prepared to provide their students with the kinds of rich experiences that their most effective K–12 teachers provided to them. Teachers already in classrooms are similarly always interested in ideas for what they can *do* differently and more effectively. Our experience tells us, then, that many readers will be glad to have arrived at this chapter, where our goal is to offer some specific and practical guidelines, examples, and resources useful in designing classroom practice.

Before moving on to those practicalities, however, we want to bring synthesis and focus to the earlier chapters by explaining the ways in which all that has come before provides context for the pedagogies we discuss here. No classroom practice can be fully effective unless a teacher accepts the ethical and legal responsibility to serve all students (Chapter One). No practice can be fully effective unless a teacher is aware of the need to resist ethnocentrism and to create a culturally inclusive classroom (Chapter Two). Moreover, unless teachers understand individual ELLs' language and literacy development in first and second languages, they cannot accurately assess students' proficiency levels, provide students with appropriate support at various phases of English language development, or identify errors that are signs of language growth (Chapters Three, Four). In short, classrooms are intensely complex environments and teaching is an intensely complex task. No teacher should ever believe that any one strategy can ensure a successful learning experience for every student, or even any one subgroup of students.

Multiple elements that affect the teaching-learning process include: classrooms full of students with inquisitive minds and diverse needs and interests; communities where students live and their parents and guardians work; rules and practices of individual schools, school districts, and states; federal mandates; and, of course, funding. Because effective teaching is born out of the interaction among these key elements and multiple contexts, what works in one context may not work in another.

Despite widespread and uninformed belief to the contrary, effective teaching is not the product of prescriptive pedagogy. Instead, it is the product of an individual teacher's professionalism, hard work and creativity. Therefore, while we trust that this chapter will provide some practical support for effective classroom activities, we urge readers to keep in mind that pedagogy is just one piece of the very complicated classroom puzzle. Good teachers have an extensive repertoire of teaching strategies, and they choose among them thoughtfully. When the strategy that worked last year doesn't work this year, they simply move on to trying another option. This chapter seeks to provide an overview of some common options.

Essentials for Any Inclusive Classroom

Although different disciplines and different grade levels obviously call for different teaching strategies, some tasks are essential for every inclusive classroom. We begin with these commonalities before moving on to considering why and how instruction must be differentiated for English language learners. As is true for all students, English language learners need to feel safe, comfortable and valued in the classroom. Therefore, teachers need to consciously craft inclusive classroom communities. In addition, since we know that mastering academic discourse adequate for their grade level can take up to seven years, teachers working with ELLs at various levels of English proficiency also should routinely plan to help them expand their vocabulary. And because (as any good student of educational psychology knows) teachers should always be strategizing to help students advance from one level of proficiency in any subject to the next, it is important for teachers of ELLs to be familiar with forms of ongoing, authentic assessment of language proficiency as well as disciplinary knowledge.

Building an Inclusive and Supportive Classroom Community

Several factors combine to create a classroom environment that nurtures student growth. These include: the teacher's insistence on respectful speech and action; predictable routines; a physical environment that acknowledges students' varied cultures; and, conscious cultivation of teacher-student and student-student relationships.

Respect. We began in Chapter One by pointing out the kinds of stereotypical and denigrating remarks that ELLs too often hear from both their peers and, unfortunately, teachers. We wish we didn't have to point out that teachers must not tolerate, let alone make, denigrating remarks to English language learners, no matter whether the speaker's intent is malicious or to be funny. At the moment, bullying is epidemic in schools at least partly because not all adults are rigorous and inflexible in forbidding verbal harassment. Refusing to tolerate such behavior is the very least teachers can do, but it is crucial. Teachers must make clear that speech and actions in the classroom are to be respectful of others, and they must model respectful speech and action themselves. For example, if a student should have a momentary lapse and say something along the lines of "What a stupid idea!" the teacher might respond both respectfully and instructively by saying something like "Oh, hang on. That can't be what you meant to say because you know we are respectful in this classroom. Did you mean to say something more like 'I'm not seeing how that would work. Can you explain more?'" Teachers need to help students learn alternatives to the insulting and hurtful discourse that often surrounds them outside the classroom. Hurtful remarks should be forbidden for *every* student.

An additional element of respect is making sure that every voice in the classroom is heard during whole class discussions. Many teachers rely on "democratic turn taking," which means that every student in the class has a turn to share her thoughts. This practice ensures that a space exists for everyone's contribution. No matter how slowly or hesitantly ELLs may speak, good teachers encourage them to finish their thoughts when it is their turn. In addition, they teach the rest of the class to be patient and to actively try to understand what their less English proficient peers may have to say. ELLs have ideas just as other students do, and their ideas deserve the same respect as others'.

Physical Environment. In addition to cultivating and modeling respect, it is relatively easy for teachers who have their own classrooms to include physical signs that multiple cultures are acknowledged and valued. Simply tacking up a map, poster or book jacket, for example, can bring a specific culture into a classroom. Posted items might include travel posters, book jackets in other languages or about other countries, or profiles of famous authors and scientists from students' home cultures. A holiday calendar, or decorations appropriate to holidays in other cultures that appear at the right time, can also make students feel included. And, we'll note here that a Jewish student might appreciate a Happy New Year sign for Rosh Hoshanah as much as a Hindu student might appreciate paper Diwali lanterns. As our title for this chapter suggests, many strategies that are good for ELLs are good for all students. Such acknowledgements in the physical environment take little effort from teachers, but they do much to create a welcoming climate for students.

Predictability. Most readers know firsthand the discomfort that arises in a situation when it's unclear what is expected. In an unfamiliar environment and among strangers, we all worry about doing or saying the wrong thing and looking foolish. Having clear and predictable classroom rules and routines can minimize such fear for ELLs by sending them clear signs about what they are expected to do at various times. Elementary teachers generally have classroom routines in place as a matter of course: students know backpacks and coats go *here*, art supplies go *there*, and that they are supposed to read the date on a calendar out loud when the teacher points to it. Secondary teachers might learn from the example of their colleagues in the lower grades. Having activities for the period listed on the board when students first enter the room, for example, can help students know that the first thing they need to do is get out their homework. For example, a list might read:

1. Homework

2. Listen. Take notes.

3. Begin new homework.

By consciously limiting and repeating the words they use in such lists, teachers can help ELLs simultaneously expand their vocabulary and respond independently with the right action at the right time. Signs for other common classroom events, like asking for a pencil, can also be helpful. A simple sign like "Need a Pencil? Raise Your Hand!"—especially with an appropriate graphic—can also help increase vocabulary and reinforce routine. After the teacher explains the sign early on, ELLs can glance at it both as a reminder of vocabulary words and of the appropriate action.

Taking care to consistently use the same words to describe the same task ("Homework, please"), or being careful to use alternative phrasings together ("Homework, please. Give me your homework") will also help ELLs navigate classroom terrain with some confidence.

Relationships. To feel part of the classroom community, ELLs must develop relationships with both their teacher and their classmates. The same kinds of relationship-building activities can be effective in both elementary and secondary classrooms. First, teachers might remember that however little English ELLs may know, they are still expert in their own culture. Creating opportunities for ELLs to comment on their own experiences and culture is one obvious and easy strategy. A teacher who brings in Diwali lanterns, for example, might ask the Hindu student to talk about how his family celebrates the holiday. In addition to creating such public opportunities, brief private conversations with a student about her personal life can also help build a relationship between student and teacher. In a casual conversation before or after instructional time, a teacher might ask about weekend plans or activities, favorite subjects, pets, or similar topics, indicating an interest in knowing the student as an individual with unique interests and experiences. Most students respond enthusiastically when they believe the teacher cares about them as people.

In addition, effective inclusive classrooms often include opportunities for collaborative work, either in pairs or in small groups. Collaboration serves several purposes. It provides an opportunity for students to get to know each other; it provides support for the English language learner because English-speaking classmates can help clarify the task; and, it provides ELLs with an opportunity to practice speaking and writing as well as listening skills. Therefore, teachers should create frequent opportunities for students to work together on tasks, allowing them to nurture positive working relationships—and possibly friendships—while simultaneously supporting content lessons and English language learning.

Examples of appropriate small group tasks include preparing for a class presentation, conducting a science experiment, brainstorming to answer a set of questions or solve a set of problems...the possibilities are endless. A typical sequence is for the teacher to provide whole group instruction, then assign collaborative tasks in small groups, and conclude with having students write individual accounts of what they learned from an activity. For example, one teacher we know provides direct instruction to explain magnetism and then gives small groups a magnet and a set of objects. After determining which objects are magnetic and which are not, students individually write what they learned about magnetic objects ("They are metal"). Teachers unfamiliar with structuring and monitoring such small group activities will find a wealth of research and advice readily available if they look for it.

Building Vocabulary

Because vocabulary is key in building language proficiency, we took time in Chapter Three to note that *knowing a word* involves knowing not only its meaning but also its sound and graphic representation. Even if ELLs can converse comfortably in English, they are likely to need help expanding their mastery of classroom vocabulary. They may need to learn abstract nouns like *principle* and *organization*, for example, or to develop an understanding of what such cognitively demanding tasks as *analyze* or *contrast* involve. Understanding such terms is obviously far more difficult than mastering concrete nouns like *book* and *friend.* Therefore, teachers working with ELLs should carefully monitor students' understanding of key academic terms and provide support in as many ways as possible.

For students with limited vocabulary, a common strategy is to pair words with objects, pictures or other illustrations. Often, teachers create (or purchase) cards linking words and pictures and have students practice saying the word on the card aloud. Elementary as well as secondary students might take such cards home for independent practice. Or, such cards might include the same word in the students' home language/s and English. They key is to provide intelligible materials that help ELLs practice words they need to know. One way to do this is to group vocabulary words by category (action words, for example, or words indicating time like *then* and *now*). Another common strategy is to encourage students to keep word study notebooks where they record words with similar spelling patterns, a practice that helps older students understand alphabetic principles in English.[1]

Labeling classroom objects is another common strategy. For example, many elementary school teachers routinely label areas of the classrooms for emergent readers, using signs like *Crayons* and *Coats* to remind students what goes where as well as to ensure they are repeatedly exposed to common vocabulary words. There is no reason secondary classrooms could not be similarly labeled with words like *homework* displayed on a basket for homework, or *microscope* attached to that instrument in a lab. When words don't correspond to a real world object, diagrams or other illustrations can be helpful. For example, *compare* might be illustrated with a drawing of something like two different cars with circles around features that look alike, as windshield wipers and license plates often do. An accompanying illustration for *contrast* might include the same two cars, but this time with differences circled: different bumpers, perhaps, or different logos and different door styles.

Since students must learn to pronounce words, effective vocabulary instruction also provides information on letter and word sounds. For example, instruction might help students learn that a final *e* is often silent (as in *bake*). Instruction also commonly targets phonograms, or letter-sound combinations. Learning the 38 phonograms[2] found in 6000 common English words allows ELLs to recognize many words immediately and to keep their focus on reading comprehension. A caution is appropriate here: we have pointed out that many readers, ELLs as well as students already proficient in English, might be able to read a text aloud without having any idea of what it means. Therefore, while ELLs certainly need instruction in pronunciation, teachers should complement lessons in sound with opportunities for students to use new vocabulary independently in their speaking and writing. In short, teachers should monitor students' performance to be sure that they have mastered all three elements—sound, meaning and spelling—of vocabulary words.

Effective vocabulary instruction should also focus on the semantic aspects of English, such as the meaning of a plural marker "s." To demonstrate plurality, teachers can again use age- and subject-appropriate pictures (one grape labeled *grape*; a bunch of grapes labeled *grape**s*** for elementary students, or similar pictures and labels for *microscope*/s in a high school science class). Middle and high school teachers can also introduce students to such learning resources as online picture dictionaries.[3]

Attentive teachers will soon learn from experience which vocabulary words are essential for ELLs to learn in their classrooms, and creative teachers will devise (or seek out) various strategies for teaching them. What is most important for teachers to remember is that as teachers of ELLs, they are *de facto* teachers of vocabulary.

Ongoing Assessment

We cannot be concerned here with the problems associated with standardized testing for ELLs, which are well known and beyond the scope of this discussion.[4] Nor does this segment address the question of how to assess an ELL's level of proficiency, a topic detailed below. Instead, in this segment we explore strategies for ongoing monitoring of student learning. Generally, what we discuss here might be best called *formative assessment*, an informal process that teachers use to monitor student performance and inform instruction. And again we note that while this is good practice for working with ELLs, it's also good standard classroom practice for all students.

To know what kind of instruction will most benefit students tomorrow, teachers must have a good understanding of where the students are today. Ongoing assessment means consciously paying attention to student performance as daily life unfolds in the classroom. Who responds to questions willingly, and how much understanding do oral responses reflect? Whose voice needs to be invited into a class discussion before it is heard? Does an ELL seem to have grasped that a prefabricated chunk she has adopted ("My family went to") can be varied ("I went to"), or might a lesson explaining that noun-verb phrase be in order? What kinds of words does a particular student use frequently, which infrequently? What kind of vocabulary instruction does that student seem to need at a particular moment? What does a particular student's question suggest about his understanding? Is he ready to work independently, or might he benefit more from being paired with another student to complete a task, or perhaps from spending some one-on-one time with the teacher?

From one perspective, we are making the common sense recommendation that teachers *pay attention* to daily life in the classroom and consciously analyze it to determine instructional strategy. Since so many elements of the classroom compete for teachers' attention, however, we know this may be a more challenging task than it may first appear. For this reason, many teachers keep a daily teaching journal, jotting down notes about classroom events as soon as possible as food for later thought. A new hesitancy on the part of a formerly outgoing student or a sudden willingness to work with others are the kinds of events that a teacher might note and analyze. Did the student hesitate because the work had reached a new level of difficulty—or did something happen to shake the student's confidence in speaking English? Has an ELL made a real friend among her classmates, making her feel more at home in the classroom—or does she need more help with today's topic than she did with yesterday's? Only by paying attention to such details of classroom life can teachers get a true picture of what is happening in the classroom and devise the most appropriate response at any given moment. We repeat: the classroom is a complex environment, and each teacher faces the daunting task of laying a new plan for tomorrow based on what happened today.

Of course, students' written work can also be monitored on an informal basis as a way to determine mastery of subject matter as well as advances in English proficiency. Almost any classroom activity will provide information on student progress if the teacher collects and retains it: learning logs, self-evaluations, charts, audio or video recordings and/or projects, drawings, concept maps, and so on. Among the resources we note in the Appendix are several books that offer ideas for formative assessment. One of the most useful aspects of such ongoing assessment is that if the teacher is paying close attention, he can address misunderstandings about a topic before they become deeply rooted. As any experienced teacher will testify, the very worst time to find out that students had a basic misunderstanding of a key topic is on a *summative assessment*, like a formal exam or a standardized test.

One particularly useful assessment strategy is the *portfolio*, which is ongoing in the sense that it includes representative student work over a particular period of time—a marking period or a school year, for example. A wide variety of portfolio models exist, including electronic as well as paper portfolios.[5] Various implementations differ greatly in design, but in general, a portfolio is essentially an intentional (as opposed to comprehensive or random) collection of student work. Unlike standardized tests that measure ELLs' discrete language and literacy skills at the moment of testing, portfolio assessment affords teachers and others opportunities to see student progress across an academic year and to understand the linkage between instruction and student learning.

For example, while a final exam might reveal whether a student knows a particular sound-letter relationship at a specific time, a portfolio might demonstrate all of the new sound-letter relationships a student had mastered *over time*. An exam provides a snapshot of what a student does or doesn't know at a particular moment, whereas a portfolio provides tangible evidence of cumulative growth. In addition, most models ask students to reflect on their learning and progress, thinking not only about what and how much they learned but also how they learned it. Typically, students explore such questions as which learning strategies were most effective for them personally, in which areas they learned most, and which areas for improvement they should concentrate on next. Teachers can also include standardized test results in student portfolios.

Many teachers discuss student portfolios with parents as well as administrators, offering those stakeholders substantive insight into both classroom instruction and areas of student growth. Given that *No Child Left Behind* mandates standardized testing for ELLs, teachers cannot protect students from test scores that may offer little useful information about the comprehensive growth they have actually experienced. However, portfolios are excellent alternative assessment tools that provide a deeper and more thoughtful portrait of student learning.

Guidelines for ELL Instruction: An Introduction to WIDA

As is true for much of this book, understanding the point we want to make about WIDA standards (defined later) requires understanding something about context. Therefore, we remind readers that in recent years (as we noted in Chapter One), schools in the United States have been strongly influenced by the widespread idea that American education can be improved through the development and implementation of standards: a blueprint for what every student should know and be able to do. As we wrote, national standards for language arts and mathematics, known as the Common Core State Standards, had been developed and adopted by 45 states and two U.S. territories and the District of Columbia. When completely implemented, the Common Core will provide the base for future standardized tests intended to measure student achievement in subject areas, including ELLs' achievement, throughout the U.S.

These standards are not the only ones shaping classroom practice, however. As *No Child Left Behind* has made clear, schools are also expected to nurture ELLs' proficiency in English. To help teachers understand what is expected in this area, several states have cooperated to support the use of standards known as WIDA (World-Class Instructional Design and Assessment). Intended to be a useful tool for teachers and schools working with ELLs, these standards help teachers and other education professionals and stakeholders identify levels of students' English language proficiency, indicating what can be expected of students at a particular level in terms of listening, speaking, reading and writing. Moreover, they provide a sketch of expectations in differing contexts, a feature particularly useful to teachers because language varies with context. That is, for example, the language of the mathematics classroom is substantively different from the language of the social studies classroom. In addition, WIDA documents offer models that demonstrate how assignments on a specific topic may be adjusted for different levels of students' English proficiency.

The WIDA standards have already been adopted by some twenty-seven states and the District of Columbia, and they are likely to become increasingly influential in the years ahead. Indeed, the standards have been written in part to provide a framework for statewide assessments. In this context, and mindful of resistance to Common Core standards, we think it wise to note openly that many teachers are understandably resistant to any educational fad *du jour* and any extrinsic control on their classrooms. They may believe that if they simply ignore standards, the standards will go away. While this has been true in the sense that many educational reforms in the past have come and gone, we believe that in this case it is actually irrelevant whether political support for the WIDA standards and for standardized testing remains or evaporates. We feel confident that no matter what happens politically, the effort to align instruction for ELLs with well-developed standards is worthwhile and can lead to substantively improved learning outcomes. While the amount of information WIDA has made available can be overwhelming on a first approach, teachers who take the time and trouble to genuinely under-

stand the WIDA documents will find them an invaluable guide for designing effective practice for ELLs.

We have no doubt that such an effort to improve practice is impera-
tive because, as we pointed out earlier, we know that many ELLs suffer
from poor educational experiences in areas where teachers, school administrators, community members, and higher educational institutions
do not have shared understanding of what good teaching for ELLs looks
like. We also know that instructional quality varies from state to state
and school to school, and that such variation can negatively affect the
future of ELLs and their families. We've seen all of this firsthand in our
work with students and schools. And, we know that research offers
much reliable knowledge about what constitutes good practice for ELLs,
but that knowledge unfortunately remains largely inaccessible to the
teachers who must design and staff effective classrooms. We believe the
WIDA standards can and should serve as an invaluable tool for teachers
struggling to make their work with ELLs both pleasant and effective.

One last point before we look more closely at the standards themselves: it's inaccurate to refer to *the* WIDA standards. Because they are
constantly being researched and refined, there are currently three versions of standards materials, produced in 2004, 2007 and 2012. The versions are complementary, however, having been developed in
succession, with each new version informed by the work and experience
that came before. Most of what we discuss below is rooted in the 2004
edition, which provided the blueprint upon which other editions build.
We turn now to that blueprint, which outlines what students should
know and be able to do in a variety of contexts.

WIDA: Standards and Levels of English Proficiency

Because teaching English in addition to teaching subject matter is an unfamiliar and daunting task for many preservice—and even inservice—
teachers, we know that a key question many readers may have is "What
exactly is it that I'm supposed to be teaching?" Without a good understanding of exactly what skills are included under the general umbrella
of English proficiency, teachers cannot adequately execute such critical
tasks as determining students' current proficiency level, designing appropriate and effective instruction, and monitoring student learning. In
detailing different areas of language use and describing proficiency lev-

els, WIDA standards help define the instructional terrain teachers inhabit across grades and in multiple subject areas.

WIDA Standards

WIDA first addresses the question of what exactly teachers are supposed to be teaching by identifying five *standards*, which essentially specify expectations for different language contexts, or for different types of discourse. [6] More specifically, Standard 1 targets language necessary for "social and instructional purposes in school settings." The other four standards state that ELLs need to "communicate information, ideas, and concepts necessary for academic success" in specific content areas. Standard 2 focuses on language arts; Standard 3, mathematics; Standard 4, science; and Standard 5, social studies. Expectations for each standard include the four domains of language use: listening, speaking, reading and writing. In the 2004 document, expectations are also sorted according to four grade clusters (K–2, 3–5, 6–8, and 9–12), but later versions are increasingly grade specific.

Levels of English Proficiency

The 2004 standards detail five levels of proficiency in English: Entering, Beginning,[7] Developing, Expanding, and Bridging.[8] Teachers can use descriptions of each level to determine students' level of proficiency. Knowing what levels their students have attained is essential for teachers to understand what kinds of learning activities are appropriate; therefore, determining proficiency level is a key preliminary task.

At the Entering Level, ELLs in K–12 grades may understand words, phrases, and frequently used word chunks; that is, for example, they may recognize a common phrase like *going to* as *gonna*. They may not, however, use such chunks voluntarily. They can understand and follow simple directions and commands when they recognize words, phrases, and word chunks in them. They can also understand pictures and graphs used in content areas such as math and science. When visual and graphic support is provided, they can understand simple statements, or simple questions that begin with who, what, how, when, why ("Where is your book?").

At the Beginning Level, ELLs can understand and use phrases and short sentences in their speech and writing. However, their oral and written language may not make sense to English speakers because of the way words are enunciated or because of unconventional word choices or sentence structure ("Can I sticker put in here?"). They can understand one-step or multiple-step directions and commands with visual and graphic support. They can also understand general language used in content areas; they might, for example, acquire such vocabulary as *beginning*, *middle*, and *end* from class study of stories.

At the Developing Level, ELLs can understand and use longer sentences in speech and writing. While their oral language and written work may still contain unconventional word choices or grammatical errors that may cause some difficulty in conveying their intended message, or while their enunciation may not be easily comprehensible, they can nevertheless generally communicate their thoughts with a small degree of visual support. They can also understand general and specific language used in content areas (like *beginning sounds* in a reading class, or *timeline* in a history class).

At the Expanding Level, ELLs can understand and use a variety of lengths of sentences and paragraphs. They can express their thoughts in oral language and written work with some errors that do not interfere with their intended message. They can understand and use specific technical language used in content areas (like *compare* and *contrast*, or *rubric*).

While some changes have been made to these descriptions since 2004, they remain a unifying force in the various versions. Again, we caution that our discussion is simply an elementary sketch of the terrain. As the following segment will illustrate, the WIDA documents offer much more guidance than may be suggested here in helping teachers understand levels of student performance.

WIDA: MPIs as Guides to Differentiated Instruction

Knowing what to teach is one thing; knowing how to teach it is something else. While teachers are now expected to help students simultaneously master subject matter and develop English proficiency, many teachers may have difficulty imagining what kinds of classroom activities might target both goals—let alone understanding how to differentiate tasks for ELLs at various levels of proficiency. This is, perhaps, where WIDA may prove most helpful to teachers. The WIDA 2007 and 2012 documents include detailed Model Performance Indicators, or MPIs. As the name suggests, these are examples of classroom tasks based on typical topics in various subject areas. A science topic illustrated for very early grades, for example, is natural resources, while for later elementary grades a topic is solar systems. Sample tasks are provided for such topics, classified both by level of proficiency and by language domains (listening, speaking, reading and writing). An enormously helpful feature of the 2007 Standards is that teachers can search the MPIs by standards, topics, language domains, and proficiency levels.[9]

A look at some model tasks may help readers get a better understanding of how these documents can help inform classroom practice.[10] The 2007 version stipulates that ELLs at the Entering Level should be able to process, understand, produce or use pictorial or graphic representation of the language of the content areas, words, phrases, or chunks of language when presented with one-step commands, directions, WH-questions, or statements with visual and graphic support (p. iii).

More simply stated, ELLs at the earliest proficiency level learn to identify and use English vocabulary words and short phrases common to classrooms and subject areas, with heavy reliance on pictures, graphs, or other illustrations. MPIs for individual standards illustrate for teachers what classroom activities aligned with this goal might look like for various subjects.

Within the subject area of language arts (Standard 2), for example, the following tasks are suggested for ELLs at the Entering level. For grades 1–2, during instruction on story sequence, a suggested reading activity is to arrange pictures into a logical sequence (p. 17); during instruction on fiction, a suggested speaking activity is to name people or objects on the illustrated cover of a book of fiction, in either L1 or L2,[11] working with a partner (p. 16). For grades 6–8, a model reading task during instruction on the genre of adventure is to identify words associated with that genre, using such supports as illustrations or word walls (p. 45); during instruction on biographies, a suggested speaking activity is to answer WH- questions based on pictures or cartoons about that genre (p. 46). For students in grades 9–12, a suggested reading activity during instruction on bias is to identify which items in a collection of illustrated phrases and sentences are facts and to share their findings with a partner (p. 59). A speaking activity on the topic of multicultural world literature is to have students offer information on literature in their home countries using visuals or graphic organizers (p. 60).

Consider the difference in tasks for students at the Expanding level. Instead of sequencing pictures, a grade 1–2 reading activity is to follow the instructions in a series of sentences that give directions for how to play a board game; a speaking activity is to offer reasons for personal likes and dislikes ("I like ___because___"), in either L1 or L2, with a partner (p. 14). A sample reading task for grades 6–8 is to pair illustrated summaries of genre types with excerpts of the genres either read aloud or presented in writing. A suggested speaking activity at that level is to summarize points about biographies presented in outlines or in graphic organizers (p. 46). For students in grades 9–12, a reading task might be to identify the author's perspective in an illustrated literary text (p. 61), and a speaking task might be to compare authors' points of view in similar stories from different cultures, using visuals or graphic organizers to support their efforts (p. 60).

In short, matrices of MPIs offer a clear illustration of the kinds of tasks appropriate for ELLs in different grades and at different levels of proficiency as they study common content topics. Because each version of the standards adds to the one before, it may take some time for teachers to find what they are looking for in the three versions. However, we believe that any time that teachers spend browsing these materials and discussing them with other teachers will do much to enhance their ability to create appropriate learning activities for ELLs in their classrooms.

Additional Resources from WIDA 2007, 2012

In addition to the useful MPI segments, the 2007 standards include a Resource Guide, which offers a wide variety of supports for teachers interested in using WIDA standards as a base to design classroom practice. Among other segments, the Guide includes examples and extended discussion of sensory supports like photographs and newspapers, graphic supports like charts and graphs, and interactive support like the use of student pairs and triads. It includes as well an explanation of *transformations*, a process for adapting model activities to local curricula. Other supports include CAN DO Descriptors for various proficiency levels, rubrics for classroom assessment of speaking and writing, sample topics for each standard, and ideas for collaboration among educators serving ELLs.

We find the 2007 WIDA standards to be the most teacher-friendly. Teachers can use the model performance indicators to assess ELLs' English proficiency levels at the beginning and end of a school year or course, a comparison that will yield information on student growth. The indicators can also provide a handy observation checklist, which teachers can use on an ongoing basis to assess growth and instructional needs. The model performance indicators further provide a scaffold on which to build instruction, with suggestions matched to subject area, proficiency level, and grade level. As the year progresses, teachers can modify the formative framework as they find necessary by adding characteristics relating to peer interactions and use of classroom technology. The framework provided by the standards can also provide a solid base for ELLs' learning portfolios, where performance on classroom tasks can be matched to standard characteristics. Of course, such assessment will also provide teachers food for thought about the effectiveness of their instruction and areas they may need to strengthen.

The 2012 standards include an amplification of ELP Standards for grades Kindergarten through 12. They include a great deal more detail on performance useful to teachers, and they feature examples of academic language, connections to state content standards—notably Common Core State Standards—and emphasis on higher-order thinking at all levels of language proficiency. Again, there is far too much to adequately summarize in this text, and readers can best understand the wealth of this and other versions of the standards by taking a look at them. All versions are online and free.

An Overview of Instructional Strategies

While WIDA offers an enormous amount of detail on specific instructional possibilities, the very quantity of detail suggests to us that it may be useful for teachers to have a more general overview of instructional strategies for ELLs to help organize their thinking. Building on her own earlier work and on Pearson's precept that teachers should gradually release responsibility for literacy learning to students, working to foster their independence,[12] Kim has devised a delineation of instructional phases keyed to WIDA proficiency levels. We offer it here for readers who may benefit from a "big-picture" snapshot of appropriate instruction for various levels. Although we make some distinctions among phases and strategies, readers should remember that at every phase it is essential that teachers maintain an encouraging and inclusive environment, provide opportunities for collaboration, and structure tasks targeting all four language domains.

Initial Phase Instruction for Entering and Early Beginning Levels

At the Entering and Early Beginning levels, teachers need to focus on helping students develop English vocabulary, with heavy reliance on pictures, drawings and other graphics to develop basic classroom vocabulary like *book*, *lunch*, *bathroom* and *open*. For example, a teacher might create a classroom poster using the simple gender drawings commonly seen on bathroom doors along with a drawing of a raised hand to help students know what to do when the need to visit the lavatory arises. In vocabulary lessons, teachers should also provide explicit information on the various ways that words may be used. For example, the word *receptacle* can mean a container or an electrical fitting, depending on the context.

Teachers also need to remember that at this level, ELLs may not respond verbally for an extended time period. Young children may be unfamiliar not only with the English language but also with the classroom and school environment. In addition, they may be anxious because of separation from their families; older children may also be struggling with the identity issues we discussed earlier. Despite ELLs' apparent lack of response, teachers should continue providing explicit English instruction, matching materials and language to students' proficiency levels and emotional maturity. That is, teachers should remember that teenagers at the earliest levels of proficiency think like teenagers, not like six-year-olds.

For example, a teacher might allow very young children to sample various fruits, tell them the name of each, and then ask which they like, or which they eat at home—questions which ELLs can answer with single words, like *apple* or *yes*. A teacher might give students in higher elementary grades an illustrated flyer from a grocery store and ask them to paste pictures of their favorite foods into a notebook and then copy words from the flyer to name and describe the pictures (*grapes*, *plump*; *steak*, *juicy*). Opportunities for high school students will vary widely with subject area. For the topic of nutrition in a health class, for example, a teacher might provide ELLs with an illustrated list of food groups and ask them to bring in pictures of common foods in their home that belong in each group, labeling each picture with its appropriate group name (*protein, fat,* and so on). In science class, when the topic is energy, the teacher might ask ELLs to bring in pictures of their families using various types of energy (someone reading by the light of an electrical lamp, someone cooking over a gas flame, and so on).

In all cases, teachers should provide generous encouragement and positive feedback as students begin attempting communication in the English language.

Intermediate Phase Instruction for Beginning and Early Developing Levels

At the Beginning and early Developing levels, ELLs can express their thoughts using basic vocabulary, and they can read simple texts. However, their oral and written expressions are marked by grammatical errors. Teachers should remember that there is a significant gap during these levels between what ELLs understand and what they can communicate, and they should make a great effort to understand what students are trying to say. Once meaning has been gleaned, teachers should model grammatical English forms central to their key ideas while concurrently providing encouragement and emotional support for their efforts.

During this phase, teachers should work to provide instruction in simplified language accessible to ELLs at these levels. Note that it is the *language* that should be simplified, not the *content.* For example, consider these lines from an online dictionary:

> The term *ecosystem* was coined in 1935, though ecosystems have been around as long as living things. *Eco* is a spin-off from the word *ecology* and describes anything having to do with the environment and our relation to it.[13]

It is unlikely that an ELL will have encountered the words *coined* and *spin-off* in the context they are used here. And, in general it is harder for readers to determine meaning in sentences when verb voice is passive than when it is active.[14] Here is what the above might look like, simplified for ELLs:

> People made the word *ecosystem* in 1935. The first part of the word, *eco*, comes from the word *ecology*. Ecology means living things and their environments.

Both versions offer the same information about the origin of the word and its derivation; the only difference is in the structure and wording of the information. It's likely, however, that ELLs would learn much more from the simplified wording than from the original.

Since the overall goal of instruction for ELLs is to advance their independence, at this phase teachers need to provide linguistic resources that ELLs can use with less support from the teacher. One example would be a personal dictionary, a place where ELLs record new words and their meanings as they encounter them. Younger children might draw pictures as definitions, while students literate in their first language might provide L1 translations and notes. Whatever system students might use, teachers should encourage ELLs to continue practicing independent learning strategies.

Elaboration Phase Instruction for Late Developing, Expanding and Bridging Levels

ELLs at this phase possess sufficient skill in English to communicate their day-to-day needs and to participate routinely in classroom activities. They may, however, still have some difficulty with very complex language structures in speech and writing. Therefore, teachers should be alert for moments of student confusion and remain ready to recast instructions and texts in simplified language as the need arises. Because students do have skills in place, teachers can help them develop strategies for monitoring their own progress. For example, teachers can call students' attention to common and persistent errors (incorrect verb endings, for example, or a consistent lack of an *s* in plural nouns) and urge them to pay special attention to checking for those errors in their writing. Again, the goal should consistently be to move from greater dependence on the teacher to more independent learning.

Because effective teaching strategies are often highly adaptable, several methods known to advance reading skills can benefit both ELLs and their mainstream classmates. We recommend three common strategies that many teachers use across grade levels and subject areas: Readers Theater, Instructional Conversations,[15] and Reciprocal Teaching.[16] In Readers Theater, students perform a dramatic reading they have rehearsed, script in hand. Unlike typical theater productions, Readers

Theater does not require props, sets, or memorization. Although the technique obviously lends itself to literary works, creative teachers have written scripts on topics ranging from polygons and global warming to the Statue of Liberty and types of sentences.[17] Performances on such topics advance both reading skills and understanding of subject matter. Many scripts are available online and for free, as are videos of student performances in grades K–12.

Instructional Conversations are discussions focused on a theme. Although they may appear to be casual conversations, teachers ensure learning by monitoring what is said and, at appropriate moments, injecting comments or questions to activate students' background knowledge, provide direct instruction, model more complex language and expressions, and nudge students to provide evidence or rationale for their statements or positions. Researchers have identified such elements as key to student learning in this format, and even teachers who already routinely hold discussions might find their skills enhanced by reading and contemplating articles on this topic like the one cited above.

Reciprocal Teaching gives students an active role in making sense of a text as it helps them develop strategies for independent reading. Teachers first model four distinct processes that readers use: summarizing, questioning, clarifying and predicting. After they understand each process, students are assigned one of the four tasks to practice in small group discussion of a text. That is, one student is responsible for summarizing (with others free to contribute), one for questioning, and so on. As they practice these roles in classroom conversations and learn strategies for dealing with difficult texts, they internalize strategies that will help them when they read independently. As is true for the other strategies, an online search will quickly yield videos showing students of various ages using the technique, from early grades through college.

This brief list does not exhaust the possibilities for useful instructional strategies, by any means. For example, WebQuests can also be useful, although teachers should be careful to create or adapt them with ELLs' needs in mind.[18] We encourage readers not to stop here, but to think through whether and how other strategies they may be familiar with might be adapted to work well with ELLs and to explore some of the many resources we've identified in the Appendix.

Summary

Good teaching for ELLs is good teaching. All teachers should provide all students with a respectful and supportive environment. They should monitor each student's learning and provide whatever form of support an individual student may need. They should provide opportunities for collaboration as well as for independent work, and they should provide opportunities to practice increasing mastery of listening, speaking, reading and writing skills. They should gradually release responsibility for learning to all students, nurturing their growth toward becoming independent, lifelong learners.

We know that differentiating instruction for ELLs at various levels of proficiency can seem a daunting task, but researchers have learned a great deal about effective ways to accomplish it. We know that visuals and vocabulary development are essential. We know that collaboration helps ELLs develop understanding of both content and literacy skills. We know that texts and oral language can be simplified and illustrated to meet the needs of ELLs at various levels, and that such support should be withdrawn gradually. It should also be reintroduced at particular moments when an ELL is flailing. We know there are well-researched instructional strategies like Readers Theater, Instructional Conversations and Reciprocal Teaching that have particular benefit for ELLs but that also are effective for every other student in the classroom.

Yes, there is much for teachers to know. And yes, it can feel overwhelming. But given the fact that teachers with internet access also have easy access to a mountain of information on instructional strategies, there really is no excuse for them not to learn what they don't know. Expertise may develop slowly, and that's understandable. But what is neither understandable nor inexcusable is any teacher's failure to make an effort to provide individual, effective instruction for ELLs whose future depends upon their academic success.

Explorations

1. Explore the internet to find scripts for Readers Theater, including scripts in content areas that would be appropriate for the grade you plan to teach. In a class discussion, share what you find as well as what you learned during your search.

2. Explore the internet to find graphics and graphic organizers appropriate for the grade level you plan to teach. In a class discussion, share what you find as well as what you learned during your search.

3. Select a paragraph of text from a book you might use in a classroom at the level you plan to teach. Rewrite the paragraph, eliminating as many complex sentences, as much passive voice, and as many idiosyncratic phrases as you can (*coined the term*, for example). Discuss the rewrites in small groups, being on the lookout for missed opportunities to simplify.

4. Try out the search feature in the WIDA materials to find a topic at the grade level you plan to teach (http://www.wida.us/standards/ELP_standardlookup.aspx). Look at Model Performance Indicators for the topic, and record sample tasks for different levels of proficiency. In small groups, discuss the tasks you identified and what they tell you about what students at various levels will need to know and be able to do in your classroom.

Notes

1   For more information on word study notebooks, please note the following reference: Helman, L., Bear., D.R., Templeton, S., Invernizzi, M., & Johnson, F. (2012). Words their way with English language learners: Word study for phonics, vocabulary, and spelling (2nd ed.). Boston, MA: Pearson Education, Inc.

2   According to the *Center for the Improvement of Early Reading Achievement Report* published in 1998, there are 38 phonograms founds in 6000 common English words. These phonograms include: at, am, ag, ack, ank, ap, an, ab, ayail, ain, ake, ell, est, ed, eed, ew, ill, op, ick, ing, in, ink, im, ight, ot, op, ob, ock, ine, out, ow, ore, unk, ug, uck, um, and y.

3   We found at least three online picture dictionaries that teachers can introduce to their students: *Merriam-Webster Visual Dictionary Online* (http://visual.merriam-webster.com/index.php) and ESOL Help Online Picture Dictionary (http://www.esolhelp.com/online-picture-dictionary.html), and *Little Explorers English Picture Dictionary* (http://www.enchantedlearning.com/Dictionary.html).

4   See, for example, Solórzano, R. W. (2008). High stakes testing: Issues, implications, and remedies for English language learners. *Review of Educational Research, 78*(2), 260–329.

5   See, for example, Barrett, H. C. (2007). Researching electronic portfolios and learner engagement: The REFLECT initiative. *Journal of Adolescent and Adult Literacy, 50*(6), 436–449. Retrieved from http://helenbarrett.com/reflect/03-JAAL-50-6Barrett.pdf.

6 All versions of WIDA Standards discussed here are available from the WIDA website, http://www.wida.us/.

7 In the 2012 edition, the Beginning level of proficiency is renamed the Emerging level.

8 Descriptions in this segment are based on the 2004 Overview document, page 6. We have, however, elaborated based on our own experience and expertise.

9 See http://www.wida.us/standards/ELP_standardlookup.aspx.

10 In this segment, sample tasks are drawn from both the 2007 and the 2012 WIDA standards, which each include multiple documents. To be clear about which document we are referencing, we include both the year and specific page numbers in the narrative. The specific 2007 documents referenced are ELP Standards PreK–Grade Five and ELP Standards Grades 6–12; the specific 2012 document referenced is WIDA 2012 Amplified ELD Standards. All documents are available from the WIDA website, http://www.wida.us/.

11 L1 and L2 designate Language One (a student's first language), L2 designates Language Two (a student's second language). In American documents, L2 generally refers to English—although for many ELLs, English may be a third or even fourth language. These designations are, however, common terms in literature discussing second language acquisition.

12 Pearson, P. D. (1985). Changing the face of reading comprehension instruction. *The Reading Teacher, 38*(8), 724–738.

13 Ecosystem. (2012). Retrieved from Vocabulary.com, http://www.vocabulary.com/dictionary/ecosystem.

14 In passive voice, something happens to the subject of the sentence, as in "The bread was baked." In active voice, the subject of the sentence does something, as in "She baked the bread."

15 Most effective teachers already use the classroom discussion strategy described here without knowing or labeling it. For a summary of Instructional Conversations, check the following website: http://www.ericdigests.org/ 1992-2/instructional.htm (retrieved October 6, 2012).

16 Reciprocal Teaching is developed as a reading instructional strategy by Annmarie Pallincsar. Note a summary of the strategy at the following website: http://www.ncrel.org/sdrs/areas/issues/students/atrisk/at6lk38.htm (retrieved on October 6, 2012).

17 See http://www.rosalindflynn.com/EdThtrScripts.html.

18 See Sox, A., & Rubinstein-Ávila, E. (2009). WebQuests for English-language learners: Essential elements for design. *Journal of Adolescent & Adult Literacy, 53*(1), 38–48.

CHAPTER SIX

The Politics of ELL Policy and Programs

What Does It Mean to Be "American"?

Many people are drawn to teaching because they believe they will be free agents in the classroom, able to draw on their own skills and creativity to meet the needs of their students. While it's true that the standards and standardized testing movement discussed in Chapter One have tightened controls on classrooms, the reality is that teachers have never had the kind of freedom that many imagine. At one time, for example, female teachers signed contracts stipulating they would wear at least two petticoats, refrain from smoking and drinking alcohol, and not leave town without permission of the school board. They were, in short, to model what the school board considered moral behavior. Later, science teachers were not allowed to discuss evolution, as the Scopes Monkey Trial famously affirmed. And in 2010, the state of Arizona banned ethnic studies courses in public schools, making courses in Mexican-American history illegal there.[1] As a result, several texts were removed from classrooms.

Because what students do and don't learn in school shapes their adult thinking and skills, various government bodies have always monitored curriculum and other parts of the school experience. This is true not only for the United States, but for all governments that provide public education. To take an obvious example, educators in democracies do not discuss possible advantages of communism, and those in communist countries do not praise democracies. In the United States, state governments are particularly influential because the federal government has no constitutional power over education. As a result, states have the right to impose their own education regulations; the Arizona ban on ethnic studies is a contemporary example. However, the federal government has used grants and other financial aid as incentives and penalties to influence school policy. In fact, it has recently wielded unprecedented power over school policy through the No Child Left Behind legislation and Race to the Top grants (as discussed in Chapter One).

Such policies are based on what politicians believe are the immediate needs of the country. They influence curriculum, and through curriculum they influence what high school graduates will know and be able to do. For example, after the Soviet Union launched the first satellite in 1957, politicians became anxious to ensure that the United States had enough scientific prowess to pull ahead and win the "space race." One result was that in 1958, Congress passed the National Defense Education Act and provided over $1 billion to schools, largely to strengthen math and science education, and colleges subsequently experienced an increase in math and science majors. As this example demonstrates, education policy is not formed in a vacuum. Instead, politicians react to specific events and devise policy in line with their goals for the future. In this case, they decided the country needed more scientists in order for the United States to dominate space exploration.

When politicians agree on state or national goals, policy decisions cause little debate. More commonly, however, they do not agree and debate policy fiercely. The question of how to educate ELLs is one that has sparked political battles for a very long time. As some researchers have pointed out, the issue is "as old as the history of immigration itself....Benjamin Franklin vocally opposed teaching German on U.S. soil, fearing that Germans would never learn English and would thus fail to become loyal Americans" (Suárez-Orozco & Suárez-Orozco, 2002, p. 136).[2] Franklin's concern has been echoed in recurring debates over the question of whether or not a "loyal American" speaks English and only English.

At its core, the debate over language policies in schools reflects a philosophical debate about what it means to be an American. When the dominant political view is that being American means speaking only English, then education policies prioritize English in classrooms. When the dominant political view is that Americans may (and perhaps should) speak more than one language, then policies make room for more than one language in classrooms. Over time events have driven policy first in one direction, then the other. At the moment, a variety of factors have once again put questions about language and language policy in the political spotlight.

Because policy drives curriculum, new policies will directly impact how tomorrow's teachers work with ELLs. And because all approaches, including the one detailed in earlier chapters of this text, reflect a particular political stance, future teachers' work with ELLs will be inescapably political. Schools do shape citizens, and teachers should understand what kind of citizens they are helping to create. To that end, this chapter first reviews key historical trends and then analyzes elements of the current context and debate. We'll close this chapter as well as this text with a final segment exploring implications of the contemporary policy debate for tomorrow's teaching professionals.

Immigration and Assimilation: Then and Now

When a situation remains the same for a very long time, people forget that things were ever different. Because there are now so many communities where everyone, or nearly everyone, speaks English, many Americans assume that it is only right and natural that instruction in public schools be in English. However, that was not always the case, and it is not universally true now.

Then

When the United States was young and expanding, and when many communities were comprised entirely of immigrants who did not speak English, it was common for public schools to use the heritage language of community members for instruction. This made perfect sense, since teachers were usually community members who often did not speak English themselves. Although contemporary Americans may find it hard to imagine a teacher speaking Swedish to a public school class, that would not have been unusual at one time. Between the 1850s and the early 1900s, several states passed laws allowing public school instruction to be wholly or partly in languages other than English. These laws allowed: "German in Pennsylvania, Maryland, Ohio, Indiana, Illinois, Missouri, Nebraska, Colorado, and Oregon; Swedish, Norwegian, and Danish in Wisconsin, Illinois, Minnesota, Iowa, North and South Dakota, Nebraska, and Washington; Dutch in Michigan; Polish and Italian in Wisconsin; Czech in Texas; French in Louisiana; and Spanish in the Southwest" (Ovando, Combs, & Collier, 2006, p. 58). [3]

Several events prompted states to change such policies. By the turn of the nineteenth century, immigrants from northern and western Europe had solidly established themselves in the United States. Not surprisingly, they began to want to share power over the country's institutions with those who had immigrated before them, challenging existing power relations. In addition, a new wave of over eight million immigrants from other parts of Europe rekindled Franklin's fear that if English weren't maintained as the country's single language, national unity would be threatened. Fears about how the new immigrants might affect the status quo spread so widely that by 1919, 15 states had designated English as the only language of instruction.[4] Rather than greeting students in their home languages, teachers began routinely punishing them for speaking anything but English in the school environment.

Such policy changes made it clear that politicians believed the job of the schools was to "Americanize" newcomer children, to make them look, sound and act like mainstream Americans. Children were to abandon all elements of their first culture and replace it with American culture in the interest of national unity. This transformational process is called *assimilation*, with the root word *similar* emphasizing that the goal is for immigrants to be remade to resemble those who came before them. The common concept of America as a melting pot reflects assimilationist goals: many different types of people may enter the U.S., but they are all expected to become one and the same once they arrive.

World War I intensified concerns about national unity, and soon after Congress passed laws that severely limited immigration from some countries and banned Asian immigration entirely. World War II also strengthened demands for national unity, even though a shortage of bilingual personnel for that war effort demonstrated that the country would benefit from having bilingual citizens. Instead of capitalizing on the skills of residents who could already speak a heritage language other than English, the 1958 National Defense Act promoted foreign language instruction for English-speaking students.

In the 1960s, however, other events began a trend away from English-only policies in schools. The decade was one of cultural upheaval as a variety of minority groups, including language minorities, came together in the Civil Rights movement to lobby for equal rights. In the same period, Congress lifted restrictions on immigration, and a flood of Cuban political refugees in Miami led to new dual language programs in schools. After bilingual schools had been established in Miami and elsewhere in Dade County, their success led other communities to make similar changes. By 1968 there were already at least 56 bilingual programs in 13 states.[5] The metaphor of melting pot was often replaced by the image of a tossed salad, with a variety of ingredients coming together to form a pleasing whole.

Federal policy moved toward valuing heritage languages when Congress passed the 1968 Bilingual Education Act, which required schools to provide special support for language-minority students who were poor; later, support was extended to all language-minority students, no matter what their socioeconomic status. This legislation was the first instance of federal support for the rights and needs of English language learners.[6] However, it was not specific about how students' needs were to be addressed, so that the question of what role heritage languages and cultures should play in federally funded programs was unsettled. The word "bilingual" suggests, however, that English was to be added on to the heritage language, not substituted for it. Reauthorizations of the Act in 1974, 1978, 1984 and 1988 reflected gradual policy shifts that aligned with shifting political concerns. Details on this evolution are beyond the scope of this text, [7] but the net result was gradual movement away from bilingualism and back toward English-only policies.

Despite this trend, two events have kept open the possibility of support for bilingual instruction, and therefore have kept open the debate about language policies for schools. The first is the 1974 Supreme Court decision in the *Lau v. Nichols* case, which found that schools receiving federal funds were required to provide language-minority students with special help; it was not specific, however, about what kind of help schools must provide. The second is that Congress passed the Equal Education Opportunity Act of 1974, which extended the *Lau* ruling to all public schools. That schools have an obligation to provide special support for English language learners is well established. What remains unclear and hotly debated is the form that support should take, and most especially what role heritage languages might, or might not, play in classrooms.

Now

As detailed in earlier chapters, recent years have seen a steady increase in the number of English language learners in public school classrooms, and that trend is expected to continue. By mid-century over half of all public school students will come from groups other than the white mainstream, including students whose first language is not English. At the same time, budget shortfalls have caused school funding to be slashed in many states, and public school administrators are struggling with budget crises. This means that just as the ELL population is doubling and tripling in many areas, administrators and teachers are being asked to do more and more with less and less. In part because providing instruction in heritage languages means hiring bilingual teachers, and because bilingual teachers are in short supply even if every school could afford them, the language policy pendulum keeps advancing toward English-only policies.

This may also be true because historically, anti-immigration sentiment follows substantive waves of immigration, when American workers fear for their jobs as well as for the theoretical unity of the culture (we say theoretical because, as we noted in Chapter Two, Americans divide themselves in many ways and on many issues). A recession beginning in 2007 has created high unemployment and triggered the worry that newcomers willing to work for low wages will take the few jobs still available away from Americans. Too often, the "unsettled anger" resulting from the stress of a poor economy becomes "a binary opposition of we/they," a perceived struggle between "the culturally homogeneous, hard-working, decent, white, long-time community members" and "racial and language minorities [and] immigrants...[perceived as] diverse, pushy, angry, ungrateful outsiders trying to get something for nothing and not caring about the basic values of the community they have invaded" (Olsen, 1997, p. 251).[8] The anger is misplaced, since there is much research to show that immigrants add to, rather than take away from, the economy.[9] For example, in 2007 one in five small businesses was immigrant-owned; overall, these small businesses employed over 4.7 million people.[10] And of course, immigrants are also consumers who pay rent or mortgages and who buy everyday necessities like food, clothing, gas and cars. However, people in economic distress themselves tend to be angry and frightened and they react not to information, but to emotions. As a result, anti-immigrant sentiment is strong in many areas.

In such a difficult economic environment, and with immigration being a sensitive political issue, it is not surprising that politicians turn away from a vision of a multilingual, multicultural country and move increasingly toward English-only policies inside and outside of the schoolhouse. With the passage of the 2001 No Child Left Behind legislation, for example, the federal Office of Bilingual Education became the Office of English Language Acquisition, Language Enhancement, and Academic Achievement for Limited English Proficient Students. Most often, the office is simply called the Office of English Language Acquisition. The shift in language reflects a shift in emphasis from educating bilingual citizens to a concern for English only. Other evidence of renewed emphasis on English acquisition comes from state laws in Massachussets, Arizona, and California, which have all passed laws mandating English-only instruction in schools.

While at one time Republicans favored English-only policies and Democrats favored bilingualism, in recent years there has been little difference between the parties on education issues, including issues of language. For example, when the Bilingual Education Act was reauthorized in 1974, Democratic Senators Edward Kennedy and Walter Mondale promoted instruction in heritage languages and cultures.[11] But no such support has been forthcoming from Democrats in recent years. In fact, echoing the language of the Republican No Child Left Behind initiative, the 2008 Democratic platform "reject[ed] the original liberal support for schools to maintain minority languages and cultures," and pledged instead "to help Limited English Proficient students get ahead by supporting and funding English Language Learner classes (Spring, 2011, p. 128)."[12] Mainstream politicians now seem to stand on the same side of the issue.

Despite this trend, many opponents to English-only programs remain, and the issue of language policy is far from settled. Many Americans still support the goals of the Civil Rights movement and still advocate minority rights, including the right to retain a heritage language. Since identity is inextricably interwoven with culture and language, abandoning a heritage language constitutes an enormous and painful loss of identity—especially when young people eventually lose the ability to converse with older family members. Opponents of English-only policies believe that educators should build on the first culture, not erase it, so that newcomers become bilingual and bicultural (instead of monolingual and monocultural). Rather than referring to Americanization as *assimilation*, they name it *deculturalization*, with the root word *culture* and the negative prefix *de* emphasizing the sacrifice of culture that assimilation requires.

In addition, they point to the fact that the United States has already absorbed wave after wave of immigrants previously feared and reviled by Americans, and it has done so without the English language or existing culture being overwhelmed. At one time, for example, many people doubted that Irish immigrants could be loyal to the United States simply because they were generally Catholic, and the Catholic Church had its own leader in the Pope. In addition, because of the extraordinary poverty which many of them endured when in Ireland, the Irish were considered not-white as well as somewhat less than human; slave owners hired them for work they considered too dangerous for their valuable slaves. Now, however, the Irish are so well-integrated that St. Patrick's Day has become a day when everyone seems to want to claim a bit of Irish heritage. Other ironies abound in the fear that other cultures will somehow overwhelm and denigrate mainstream culture. For example, in contemporary America, the over-stressed American, so sure of having the best of all possible cultures, often spends large sums of money to learn to relax using the ancient Eastern arts of meditation and yoga.

History truly does repeat itself, since it offers multiple examples of Americans fearing new immigrant groups that, in time, were seamlessly woven into the fabric of the United States, despite popular fears. As was true in Franklin's time, the debate about language policies in schools is just one part of the much larger debate about how to define "an American" and what the United States will look and sound like in the future. Will Americans be monolingual or bilingual (or multilingual)? Will they be monocultural or bicultural (or multicultural)? The answers to those questions will drive language policies, which in turn will drive curriculum. Teachers, therefore, will promote the development of one type citizen over the other, whether they are aware of doing it or not, and whether they agree with the vision underpinning policy or not.

Limitations of This Discussion

Readers should be aware that this brief and superficial discussion of ideology omits many topics relevant to the politics of educating English language learners. Not only in the United States, but in many countries, language issues routinely provoke heated debate. As Suárez-Orozco & Suárez-Orozco point out in their 2001 study of immigrant children:

> That language should be the topic of emotional and politicized debate should not surprise anyone. While on the surface language is about communication, it is also a marker of identity and an instrument of power. The United States is not alone in ex-

periencing tensions regarding bilingualism and second-language policy. While some countries such as Switzerland have worked out successful multilingual arrangements, other countries continue to struggle with this issue .... (p. 135) [13]

The issues around language policy in schools have far greater depth than is evident in the above discussion.

We have not, for example, discussed the idea embraced by both political parties and most of the American public that the primary purpose of public schools is to help fuel the economy by educating workers to the specifications of the business community. Not the welfare of children, but the welfare of business is driving contemporary policy discussions and decisions—and for ELLs, education for work has come to mean education *as* English-speaking workers, a task to be accomplished as quickly and cheaply as possible. A second topic we have not addressed is the role that poverty plays in achievement gaps between many English language learners and their mainstream counterparts from middle class communities. When English language learners are poor, they attend poor schools that often don't receive the resources necessary to even begin to compensate for known effects of poverty. Directly related to this point is a third topic we have not touched on: the way that the current funding of public schools reinforces existing power relationships, so that power and wealth remain in the same few hands.

These are all critical topics, and they all influence the experiences of English language learners in schools. Each has been the subject of intensive research, and each has proponents of and opponents to the above assertions. Despite their importance, however, they lie beyond the scope of this text, which has as its main purpose to explain a particular pedagogical strategy while simply alerting readers that politics play an enormous role in school policy, and especially in policy for ELLs. Tomorrow's teachers would be well advised to undertake the additional reading and study necessary to develop a much deeper understanding of the politics of educational policy than this brief text can hope to provide.[14]

From Politics to Policy and Programs: A Tower of Babel

We've already pointed out that language matters. When the words *bilingual education* were replaced by references to *English language acquisition* in federal policy, the language reflected a conscious shift of emphasis away from bilingualism and toward English-only policies. Understanding the import of language choices can help teachers better understand the political context of their work environment, because terminology signals the assumptions and goals of particular people, policies and programs.

Terms to Describe Students

How to even name students who need to learn English has been a matter of debate because connotations vary so widely. We have used the term *English language learners* consistently throughout this text, and we have done so for a reason. Specifically, we believe the term suggests an emphasis on students as learners and names a subject they are working to master. In using *English language learners*, we have also consciously avoided another widely used term: *Limited English Proficiency*, or *LEP*. This designation comes from federal legislation, and so it is widely used. However, many educators dislike it because it seems to define students entirely by what they lack—a command of English—and creates what is known as a *deficit model* of students. That is, the term suggests that what is most important about the students is what they don't yet know. It portrays the students as a problem population that needs to be fixed, that is faulty. In that sense, the term reflects a concern for assimilation and an English-speaking population.

However, there are still others who would object to our use of the term *English language learners* because they believe it defines the students only in terms of their language abilities and fails to emphasize the richness of the cultures they bring to the classroom with them. To call attention to these students' assets, and to promote diversity as normal, some writers use the broadly inclusive term *Culturally and Linguistically Diverse*, or *CLD*. While we agree that students' cultures are valuable and contribute both to student learning and classroom life, we have not used this term because it includes students other than those we are focusing on. More specifically, many educators who work with African-American (or Black) students argue that their culture varies substantively from dominant culture and that teachers need to use culturally appropriate strategies with these students as well. In this book, we have instead focused only on students whose first language is not English, making the use of CLD inaccurate for our discussion, even though we share the perception of diversity as a resource rather than a threat.

Still others argue for terminology making clear the strengths that students will emerge with if they master English and maintain proficiency in their home language as well: *Emergent Bilinguals.* We believe there is much to be said for the positive connotations of this term, but some political risk to using it since the term *bilingual* is politically charged and under attack at the moment, as we'll discuss below.

Here or there, we have referred to ELLs as *newcomers* and to dominant culture as *mainstream*, and these are also terms others criticize. We use *newcomer* as a more general term than *immigrant* because many English language learners are in the United States temporarily. Often, foreign professionals will work for some years in the United States to expand their professional experience but with no intention of remaining. Their children often appear in public schools in the population known as *English language learners.* To use the term *immigrants* for all students learning English is, therefore, inaccurate. It's possible we have allowed a bit of inaccuracy to slip into our discussion in any event, however, since all ELLs are not recently arrived and not technically "newcomers."

In addition, we have used the term *mainstream* to indicate dominant culture. We have avoided the term *dominant* because it offends some people who think it suggests that the strongest culture willfully oppresses others. However, others object to the use of *mainstream* because they believe it sets English language learners apart as "not mainstream" and therefore "not normal"—the same problem we explored at length in Chapter Two.

Our purpose here is not to make readers throw up their hands and say "Well, no matter *what* language I use, someone is going to object." That may be true, but it's not the point. Instead, the point is to emphasize yet again that language matters. It often reflects a particular stance toward learners, and how learners are defined influences the strategies that are prescribed for them. Educators are called on to *fix* students with limited proficiency, but they are called on to help *nurture* emergent bilinguals. Paying attention to language will help teachers understand the politics and intentions operating in their environment. And, this is true not only for language used to describe learners themselves, but also for language used to describe policy and programs that determine their fate in schools.

Terms to Describe Programs and Pedagogies

As we noted above, for some people, the goal of schooling is Americanization, or total assimilation, while for others the goal is a bilingual (or multilingual) and diverse society. Obviously, heritage languages will play a key role in the classroom when the goal is bilingualism, and less and less of a role as the goal moves closer and closer to English-only emphasis. The *Lau* ruling forbids the option at the extreme end of the English-only policy spectrum, which is *submersion*. Also known as *sink-or-swim, submersion* places ELLs into a mainstream classroom with no support whatever. While *Lau* rules out that option, a range of possibilities remains because the ruling specifies neither a specific goal nor any particular type of support. As a result, multiple approaches to working with English language learners have developed, with a nearly bewildering range of terms to describe them.

It can be particularly challenging to sort through terms for programs because terminology is not consistent; the same term can be used to describe substantively different programs. For example, although the term *bilingual* is used in the name of several approaches, it is used to describe programs that do pursue bilingualism as well as those that don't. *Transitional Bilingual* or *Early Exit Bilingual* programs, for example, allow the students' heritage language to be used briefly to help them with academic content while they are also learning English. However, the goal of the approach (indicated by the term *early exit*) is to move students into regular classrooms and English-only instruction as quickly as possible. Once students leave the program, there is no instruction in or use of their heritage language. In contrast, *Developmental Bilingual* or *Late Exit Bilingual* programs provide instruction in the heritage language as well as in English over an extended time period, allowing students to develop literacy as well as academic content knowledge in both languages.

An emphasis on bilingualism is even more pronounced in *Bilingual Immersion* programs, which are also known as *Two-Way Immersion* or *Dual Language* programs, with the term "dual language" perhaps intended to avoid the antipathy that the word "bilingual" provokes among some groups. As one researcher summarizes,

> Bilingual education has basically become a dirty word, but dual-language programs seem to have this cachet that people are glomming onto...white, middle-class par-

ents want these programs to give their children an edge in the increasingly global-
ized world. (Sugarman as cited in Wantanabe, 2011) [15]

In these programs, instruction is provided both in English and in a second language, and the explicit goal is competence in both languages. Often, as indicated above, these programs are designed not for ELLs but for
middle-class American parents who want their children to learn a language other than English to in order to have an edge in the job market.

Dual language programs do not, however, serve only middle-class
students. When a school has a large population of ELLs who speak the
same heritage language, a dual-language program may enroll half English-speaking students and half ELLs. In such cases, the ELLs learn English as their English-speaking counterparts learn their heritage language.
Instruction is provided in both languages, and students use both languages in the classroom. Most often there are two teachers with each
using a different language for instruction, although the teachers may
well be bilingual themselves. While Spanish-English programs are most
numerous, there are also many programs using other languages, including Mandarin Chinese, Japanese, Korean, German, and French. Such programs promote a bilingual citizenry, no matter whether their intended
purpose is to give English-speaking students an edge in the job market
or to affirm and value the diverse languages and cultures that ELLs bring
to American classrooms.

Another imprecise term is *English for Speakers of Other Languages*,
or *ESL*. Typically, students in an ESL program study English as a subject,
much as English-speaking students study foreign languages in high
school and college classes. Lessons focus on grammar (verb conjugation,
for example), vocabulary and other elements of the language, and the
goal is to support students so that they can benefit from regular classroom instruction in English. What makes this terminology particularly
confusing is that *any* approach, bilingual or otherwise, typically includes
the same kind of instruction as an ESL class. All forms of language teaching provide instruction in formal elements of the language, and it would
be a mistake to think that a program labeled *bilingual* would not include
such instruction.

Structured Immersion, or *Sheltered Immersion* programs, like dual-
immersion programs, have been steadily increasing in popularity.
Though the terms are often used interchangeably, each refers to differ-

ent strategies and it would be better not to conflate them. However, in practice these two strategies are typically used together, and one term or the other is used to reference the overall program. *Structured immersion* means that ELLs spend much of their school day studying English as a formal subject, grouped by proficiency level and with lessons provided in English. The goal is for ELLs to learn English as rapidly as possible and to continue studying it until they are proficient in academic language, not just in conversation. Students do, however, spend some time in regular classes in subject areas, where teachers speak English but use *sheltered immersion* (or *content-based instruction*). This means that teachers in regular classes adapt their classroom language and lessons in ways that make them accessible to students who are not yet proficient in English.

Readers will, we trust, recognize that this text details strategies for sheltered, or content-based, immersion. However, it is possible that our work suggests greater emphasis on heritage languages and cultures than many immersion programs intend. This is true for several reasons. First, some states have recognized that ignoring student culture can impede learning, and so they have included knowledge of culture in their standards for teacher education. Second, valuing the home culture and language of students is sound pedagogy. For example, all students retain new information better when teachers link it to something familiar. In addition, students need to feel at home in a classroom so that they feel safe taking risks, allowing teachers to see their misunderstandings and weaknesses and to help students overcome them. An inclusive classroom where everyone's experience is valued provides a maximum learning environment for every student in it.

There is, then, some room in a sheltered immersion approach for teachers to honor their students' languages and cultures. It is highly unlikely, however, that the design of any structured immersion program will include a significant role for students' heritage. States are increasingly mandating a structured immersion approach in part because of anti-immigrant sentiment and a subsequent backlash against bilingual education; the goal of the approach is seemingly the assimilationist goal of efficient mastery of English. Unless individual teachers choose to give students' heritage languages and cultures more than a token, instrumental role in the classroom, the sheltered immersion approach is likely to advance the goal of a monolingual, monocultural society.

What Does Research Say about Alternative Approaches?

Before looking to research to provide definitive answers on such complex questions as which pedagogy works best with English language learners, it is important to understand the limitations of educational research. First, because there is no uniform group of "English language learners"—just as there is no uniform group of "third graders" or any other student group—that question does not and cannot have a single definitive answer. For example, it is unlikely that the approach that works best with a highly motivated Japanese student already literate in Japanese would also be the approach that works best with a first grade student from Afghanistan who had never attended school and whose parents were illiterate.

Second, it is difficult to say what a particular approach has or hasn't accomplished, because various approaches may be implemented very differently by different people in different places. Many factors affect how successful a particular teacher or school may be in working with ELLs. For example, teachers may have had extensive—or no—training in an approach mandated for their classrooms. They may have been given extensive support and resources to help develop materials for their classroom—or they may have lacked even basic supplies. Their students may all have spoken the same heritage language—or they may have spoken half a dozen or more different languages. Their students may be accomplished readers and writers in their first language—or they may not have had access to paper and writing utensils. Their students may have come to school in clean new clothes having had a hearty, nourishing breakfast—or they may have had little or nothing to eat since a scant dinner the evening before.

In short, although many public voices currently insist that if students fail the fault must lie with the teacher or with the pedagogical approach, cause and effect for student success and failure are not so easily determined. Each classroom situation is different from every other classroom situation. A particular approach may work well in one context and fail miserably in another, or it may work well in the hands of one teacher and dismally in the hands of another. Because teaching is a human activity and humans are so variable, grandiose claims about *the* best thing for every student in every classroom are never justified.

It is no surprise, then, that different studies on different approaches should have different findings. The issue is, however, clouded more by political stances than by the research itself:

> Because in the United States the notion of bilingual education itself is so politically loaded, research about the question of whether bilingual education, or monolingual, English-only education works best for emergent bilinguals is often contradictory. Nevertheless, and on balance, there is much research support for the positive effects of bilingual education over monolingual education for these students. (Garcia & Kliefgen, 2010, pp. 48–49) [16]

Researchers have identified several specific benefits of bilingual instruction that persuade many that it is the strongest approach. Allowing students to use their heritage language helps them transfer what they know about language use in one language to another, no matter whether their first language shares many or few characteristics with English. For example, a teacher may call Spanish-speaking students' attention to the way verb endings change in Spanish, making a lesson in English verb conjugation more accessible. Or, students who had learned to read in Chinese would already know that the job of a reader is to make sense of marks on a page, and that texts are read starting in one place and moving in a particular direction. Simply stated, heritage languages can provide a ready springboard, or platform, to facilitate students' understanding of the structure of English.

As has been the case for the many topics squeezed into this relatively brief text, the above is an oversimplification of the greatest magnitude of what is known about bilingual education and bilingualism. Language is an extremely complex process, and researchers have developed extremely detailed and nuanced understandings of human communication. Therefore, we again urge readers to undertake far more extensive study, especially in educational linguistics.

Even a better understanding of the research base supporting bilingual education, however, will not change policies in place. Political decisions are rarely, if ever, based on honest, disinterested research. Moreover, even if the political current suddenly reversed itself to support bilingual education, many communities would be unable to adequately fund it, and far too few bilingual teachers are available. What is the overall picture, then, for tomorrow's teachers in tomorrow's schools?

> What is evident from the research is that the use of the student's home language is crucial for their long-term cognitive growth and academic achievement in English. And thus, all teachers, those who are required to deliver instruction in English only and those who do so bilingually, can take a more effective pedagogical path by constructing bilingual instructional spaces. (Garcia & Kliefgen, 2010, p. 50) [17]

Individual teachers may need to be resourceful in creating such spaces, but there is every reason to believe that the better able they are to do so, the better their ELLs will be able to learn.

A Closing Thought on Professionalism: Who Will You Be Tomorrow?

Teachers working with thirty or more students in a classroom and frustrated by the mandates of high stakes testing that seem to dominate their classrooms typically believe they have little time for such "ivory tower" concerns as philosophy. The questions of "What language policy best serves English language learners?" and "What do I think the United States should look like tomorrow?" seem very far removed from pragmatic questions like "What am I going to do in class on Monday morning?" And yet, whether they will it or not, teachers do in fact every day help shape the citizenry of tomorrow. Since everyone seems to want to say what those citizens should be like, teachers will find that their efforts are pushed first one way and then pulled another by competing stakeholders including parents, administrators, politicians, corporations and students themselves. The danger in *not* thinking about philosophy and related policy questions is that teachers may unconsciously advance an agenda that they would not support—had they ever stopped to think about it.

Nothing is inevitable and any policy can be changed. But: the future is shaped by those who act. If teachers don't like the present, or if they want to have a say in the future, then they have no choice but to inform themselves on issues, take an informed position, and then *act* to try to shape the future. To do nothing is to choose to simply go along with what others decide.

Our one-time colleague, Bridget Bunten, had a painful lesson in this reality. Bridget had only just begun a job as a bilingual teacher in Massachusetts when voters passed a ballot initiative in favor of an English-only policy for schools. The two-way immersion program she had been hired to teach in was derailed, and she watched as instruction was to-

tally transformed in the school in a very few years—and not, she believed, for the better. Her experience is, unfortunately, typical for too
many teachers.

> During the hours that I spent at the school in preparation for the first day, not once
> was I involved in a conversation with colleagues that mentioned the upcoming elec-
> tions in November or the possibility that our Two-Way program could not exist in a
> year. Looking back, I am disappointed in myself for not being more politically aware
> about a proposed law that would directly impact my coveted teaching position.
> (Bunten, 2009, pp. 4–5)[18]

While the teachers may have discussed the issue from time to time as
campaigning for an English-only policy intensified, the teachers never
met as a body to think through the implications of the initiative or to
strategize in any way to defend a program that several teachers believed
in passionately. Only after the program was totally dismantled and
structured English immersion implemented did Bridget realize advocacy
as a professional responsibility: "Prior to beginning my professional experience at [this school], I hadn't fully considered what it meant to be a
teacher in order to advocate for children, influence policy, and be politically involved" (Bunten, 2009, p. 11).[19] Only when it was too late did she
realize that if teachers don't want decisions made by outsiders, they
must act to shape policy decisions.

Bridget also left the experience understanding that even in a highly
restrictive policy environment, teachers have a responsibility to find
ways to do what is truly best for students in the classroom.

> The five years that I spent teaching and learning from ELLs, their parents, and my
> colleagues helped me realize that teachers play an important role in interpreting
> and shaping policy at the classroom level. Even if there are instances when we feel
> that our hands our tied and we must follow along, teachers have the autonomy to
> made instructional decisions that are in the best interests of their students rather
> than those of the 'outsiders.' (Bunten, 2009, pp. 11–12)[20]

However little room there may be to maneuver, ethical teachers *will* do
their best for students, no matter the policy environment that circum-
scribes their classroom.

Teachers who believe they can remain neutral and unengaged in
politics simply by doing nothing (except what they are told to do) both
delude themselves and cheat children of their support. To do nothing

but follow along *is* to choose: it is to choose to allow others to decide. Teachers make a choice, consciously or not, either to *act* as an advocate for children and engage in political action—or to do nothing but plod along on a course determined by others.

It is our fervent hope that you will choose to act. Professionalism demands—and your students will need—your best efforts in creating classrooms that serve all students well and that shape a citizenry for our most hopeful vision of the future.

Explorations

1. The idea of serving as advocate and becoming politically involved is a new one for many teachers and future teachers. Let your imagination explore this territory to help you visualize the kind of professional you may become. Can you imagine yourself being politically active as policy is being shaped? What dispositions would that require? Do you have those dispositions? If not, could you cultivate them? How?

2. Actions have consequences. What are the benefits and risks of political advocacy? What are the benefits and risks of rejecting the role of advocate?

3. Explore policies in your state relevant to educating English language learners. Who supports the policies? Why? Who opposes them? Why? Which camp are you aligned with? Why?

4. Name one thing you might do right now in your state as a first step toward advocacy.

Notes

1   Somanader, T. (2012, January 12). School suspends Mexican-American history program to comply with Arizona's ban on ethnic studies. Retrieved July 12, 2012, from http://thinkprogress.org/justice/2012/01/12/403118/school-suspends-mexican-american-history-program-to-comply-with-arizonas-ban-on-ethnic-studies/

2   Suárez-Orozco, C., & Suárez-Orozco, M. M. (2002). *Children of immigration.* Cambridge, MA: Harvard University Press.

3   Ovando, C.J., Combs, M. C., & Collier, V. P. (2006). *Bilingual and ESL classrooms: Teaching in multicultural contexts.* Boston: McGraw-Hill.

4   Ovando, C.J., Combs, M. C., & Collier, V. P. (2006). *Bilingual and ESL classrooms: Teaching in multicultural contexts.* Boston: McGraw-Hill.

5   Ovando, C.J., Combs, M. C., & Collier, V. P. (2006). *Bilingual and ESL classrooms: Teaching in multicultural contexts.* Boston: McGraw-Hill.

6   Ovando, C.J., Combs, M. C., & Collier, V. P. (2006). *Bilingual and ESL classrooms: Teaching in multicultural contexts.* Boston: McGraw-Hill.

7   For a detailed discussion of how and why policy for the instruction of ELLs has evolved in the ways it has, readers are advised to consult Chapter 2 of the Ovando, Combs and Collier text cited above, to which we are indebted for much of this historical information, as indicated.

8   Olsen, L. (1997). *Made in America: Immigrant students in our public schools.* New York: The New Press.

9   ACLU. (2002, March 12). Immigrants and the economy. Retrieved July 21, 2012, from http://www.aclu.org/immigrants-rights/immigrants-and-economy

10   Immigration Policy Center. (2012, June). Strength in diversity: The economic and political power of immigrants, Latinos, and Asians in the U.S. Retrieved July 24, 2012, from http://www.immigrationpolicy.org/sites/default/files/docs/Strength%20in%20Diversity%20updated%2006061912.pdf

11   Spring, J. (2011). *The politics of American education.* New York: Routledge.

12   Spring, J. (2011). *The politics of American education.* New York: Routledge.

13   Suárez-Orozco, C., & Suárez-Orozco, M. M. (2002). *Children of immigration.* Cambridge, MA: Harvard University Press.

14   Readers interested in such a discussion should consult the Joel Spring text referenced above, which provides a detailed and clear picture of contemporary American politics. There is no shortage of research detailing the impact of poverty on poor schools and students, as the most cursory internet search will reveal.

15   Julie Sugarman of the Center for Applied Linguistics, quoted in Wantanabe, T. (2011, May 8). Dual-language immersion programs growing in popularity. *Los Angeles Times.* Retrieved July 21, 1202, from http://articles.latimes.com/2011/may/08/local/la-me-bilingual-20110508

16   Garcia, Ó., & Kleifgen, J. A. (2010). *Educating emergent bilinguals: Policies, programs, and practices for English language learners.* New York: Teachers College Press.

17   Garcia, Ó., & Kleifgen, J. A. (2010). *Educating emergent bilinguals: Policies, programs, and practices for English language learners.* New York: Teachers College Press.

18   Bunten, B. A. (2009). *A previous teacher's autobiographical examination of her experiences with an English-only policy.* Unpublished manuscript.

19   Bunten, B. A. (2009). *A previous teacher's autobiographical examination of her experiences with an English-only policy.* Unpublished manuscript.

20   Bunten, B. A. (2009). *A previous teacher's autobiographical examination of her experiences with an English-only policy.* Unpublished manuscript.

APPENDIX

Resources for the Classroom Teacher of English Language Learners

Books for Classroom Practice

Ariza, E. N. (2010). *Not for ESOL teachers: What every classroom teacher needs to know about the linguistically, culturally, and ethnically diverse student* (2nd ed.). Boston, MA: Allyn & Bacon.

Bear, D. R., Helman, L., Templeton, S., Invernizzi, M., & Johnson, F. (2007). *Words their way with English learners: Word study for phonics, vocabulary, and spelling instruction.* Upper Saddle River, NJ: Pearson Merrill Prentice Hall.

Beck, I. L., McKeown, M. G., & Kucan, L. (2008). *Creating robust vocabulary: Frequently asked questions and extended examples.* New York, NY: Guilford Press.

Coppola, J. (2009). *Teaching English language learners in Grades K-3: Promoting language and literacy development.* Norwood, MA: Christopher-Gordon Publishers.

Coppola, J., & Primas, E.V. (Eds.). (2009). *One classroom, many learners: Best literacy practices for today's multilingual classrooms.* Newark, DE: International Reading Association.

Cruz, B. C., & Thornton, S. J. (2009). *Teaching Social Studies to English language learners.* New York, NY: Routledge.

Dacey, L., & Gartland, K. (2009). *Math for all: Differentiating instruction, Grades 6-8.* Sausalito, CA: Math Solutions.

Díaz-Rico, L.T. (2013). *Strategies for teaching English learners* (3rd ed.). Boston, MA: Pearson.

Echevarria, J., Vogt, M., & Short, D. J. (2013). *Making content comprehensible for English learners: The SIOP model* (4th ed.). Boston, MA: Pearson.

Freeman, Y. S., Freeman, D. E., & Ramírez, R. (Eds.) (2008). *Diverse learners in the mainstream classroom: Strategies for supporting all students across content areas.* Portsmouth, NH: Heinemann.

Hadaway, N. L., & Young, T. A. (2010). *Matching books and readers: Helping English learners in grades K-6.* New York, NY: Guilford Press.

Haussamen, B., Benjamin, A., Kolln, M., & Wheeler, R. S. (2003). *Grammar alive!: A guide for teachers.* Urbana, IL: National Council of Teachers of English (NCTE).

Helman, L., Bear, D. R., Templeton, S., Invernizzi, M., & Johnston, F. (2012). *Words their way with English learners: Word study for phonics, vocabulary, and spelling (*2nd ed.*).* Boston, MA: Pearson.

Herrell, A. L, & Jordan, M. (2012). *50 strategies for teaching English language learners* (4th ed.) Boston, MA: Pearson.

Herrera, S. G., Perez, D. R., & Escamilla, K. (2010). *Teaching reading to English language learners: Differentiated literacies.* Boston, MA: Allyn & Bacon.

Hiebert, E. H., Pearson, P. D., Taylor, B. M., Richardson, V., & Paris, S. G. (1998). *Every child a reader: Applying reading research in the classroom.* Ann Arbor, MI: Center for the Improvement of Early Reading Achievement (CIERA), University of Michigan School of Education.

Jenkins, J. (2009). *World Englishes: A resource book for students* (2nd ed.). New York, NY: Routledge.

Kennedy, G. (2003). *Structure and meaning in English: A guide for teachers.* Harlow, England: Pearson Longman.

Kersaint, G., Thompson, D. R., & Petkova, M. (2009). *Teaching mathematics to English language learners.* New York, NY: Routledge.

Kress, J. E. (2008). *The ESL/ELL teacher's book of lists* (2nd ed.) San Francisco, CA: Jossey-Bass.

Lessow-Hurley, J. (2013). *The foundations of dual language instruction* (6th ed.). Boston, MA: Pearson.

Levine, L. N., & McClosky, M. L. (2013). *Teaching English language and content in mainstream classes: One class, many paths* (2nd ed.). Boston, MA: Pearson.

O'Malley, J. M., & Pierce, L.V. (1996). *Authentic assessment for English language learners: Practical approaches for teachers.* Reading, MA: Addison-Wesley Publishing Company, Inc.

Parker, E., & Pardini, T. (2006). *"The words came down!": English language learners read, write, and talk across the curriculum, K-2.* Portland, ME: Stenhouse Publishers.

Peregoy, S. F., & Boyle, O.F. (2012). *Reading, writing, and learning in ESL: A resource book for teaching K-12 English learners* (6th ed.). Boston, MA: Pearson.

Reiss, J. (2008). *102 content strategies for English language learners: Teaching for academic success in grades 3-12.* Upper Saddle River, N.J: Pearson/Merrill/Prentice Hall.

Reiss, J. (2012). *120 content strategies for English language learners: Teaching for academic success in secondary school* (2nd ed.). Boston, MA: Pearson/Allyn and Bacon.

Short, D. J., Vogt, M., & Echevarria, J. (2011). *The SIOP model for teaching science to English learners.* Boston, MA: Pearson.

Tiedt, P. L. & Tiedt, I. M. (2002). *Multicultural teaching: A handbook of activities, information, and resources* (6th ed.). Boston, MA: Allyn and Bacon.

Books for Understanding Learners, Parents, and Immigrant Communities

Bissex, G.L. (1980). *Gnys at wrk: A child learns to write and read.* Cambridge, MA: Harvard University Press.

Connery, M. C. (2011). *Profiles in emergent biliteracy: Children making meaning in a Chicano community.* New York, NY: Peter Lang.

Lyons, M., & Tarrier, A., (Eds.) (2009). *Mirrors and windows: Oral histories of Mexican farmworkers and their families.* New City Community Press & Syracuse University Press.

Olsen, L. (1997). *Made in America: Immigrant students in our public schools.* New York, NY: New Press.

Portes, A., & Rumbaut, R. G. (2001). *Legacies: The story of the immigrant second generation.* Berkeley, CA: University of California Press.

Santa-Ana, O. (Ed.) (2004). *Tongue-tied: The lives of multilingual children in public education.* Lanham, MD: Rowman & Littlefield Publishers, Inc.

Suárez-Orozco, C., & Suárez-Orozco, M. M. (2001). *Children of immigration.* Cambridge, MA: Harvard University Press.

Valdés, G. (2001). *Learning and not learning English: Latino students in American schools.* New York, NY: Teachers College Press.

Books for Explorations in Linguistics, Literacy, Philosophy, and Psychology

August, D., Hakuta, K., & National Research Council (U.S.). (1998). *Educating language-minority children.* Washington, D.C: National Academy Press.

Austin, J. L. (1962). *How to do things with words: The William James lectures delivered at Harvard University in 1955.* New York, NY: Oxford University Press.

Bialystok, E. & Hakuta, K. (1994). *In other words: The science and psychology of second-language acquisition.* New York, NY: Basic Books.

Brown, R. (1973). *A first language: The early stages.* Cambridge, MA: Harvard University Press.

Cazden, C. B. (1988). *Classroom discourse: The language of teaching and learning.* Portsmouth, NH: Heinemann.

Chomsky, N. (1965). *Aspects of the theory of syntax.* Cambridge, MA: M.I.T. Press.

Cleary, L. M., & Linn, M. D. (1993). *Linguistics for teachers.* New York, NY: McGraw-Hill.

Cook, V. (1993). *Linguistics and second language acquisition.* New York, NY: St. Martin's Press.

Dewey, J. (1916). *Democracy and education: An introduction to the philosophy of education.* New York, NY: The Free Press.

Dewey, J. (1997). *Experience and education.* New York, NY: Touchstone.

Emerson, C., & Holoquist, M. (Eds.). (1986). *M. M. Bakhtin: Speech genres and other late essays.* Austin, TX: University of Texas Press.

Halliday, M. A. K., & Hasan, R. (1989). *Language, contexts, and text: Aspects of language in a social-semiotic perspective.* Oxford: Oxford University Press.

Hinchey, P.H. (2008). *Action research: Primer.* New York, NY: Peter Lang.

Philips, S. U. (1983). *The invisible culture: Communication in classroom and community on the Warm Springs Indian reservation.* New York, NY: Longman.

Skinner, B. F. (1957). *Verbal behavior.* New York, NY: Appleton-Century-Crofts.

Tomlinson, C. A., Brimijoin, K., & Narvaez, L. (2008). *The differentiated school: Making revolutionary changes in teaching and learning.* Alexandria, VA: ASCD.

Book Chapters for Classroom Practice

Arrowood, J. C. (2004). Putting it all together. *Mathematics for ESL Learners* (pp. 131–192). Lanham, MD: Scarecrow Education.

Cummins, J. (1994). The acquisition of English as a second language. In K. Spangenberg-Urbschat & R. Prichard (Eds.), *Kids come in all languages: Reading instruction for ESL students* (pp. 36–62). Newark, DE: International Reading Association.

Orellana, M. F., & Hernández, A. (2003). Talking the walk: Children reading urban environmental print. In P. M. Mason & J. S. Schumm (Eds.), *Promising practices for urban reading instruction* (pp. 25–36). Newark, DE: International Reading Association.

Journal Articles for Classroom Practice

Parhar, N., & Sensoy, Ö. (2011). Culturally relevant pedagogy redux: Canadian teachers' conceptions of their work and its challenges. *Canadian Journal of Education, 34*(2), 189–218. Retrieved from http://search.proquest.com/docview/881643998?accountid=13158

Pearson, P. D. (1985). Changing the face of reading comprehension instruction. *The Reading Teacher, 38*(8), 724–738.

Sox, A., & Rubinstein-Ávila, E. (2009). WebQuests for English-language learners: Essential elements for design. *Journal of Adolescent & Adult Literacy, 53*(1), 38–48.

Online Resources

Assessing Children's Literature (Anti-Defamation League)
   http://www.adl.org/education/assessing.asp

Bilingual/English as a Second Language (ESL) Education (Connecticut Department of Education)
   http://www.sde.ct.gov/sde/cwp/view.asp?a=2618&q=320848&sdeNavPage=%7C

Bilingual/ESL Program (Wisconsin Department of Public Instruction)
   http://ell.dpi.wi.gov/

Bureau of Student Achievement Through Language Acquisition (Florida Department of Education)
  http://www.fldoe.org/aala/

¡Colorín Colorado!
  http://www.colorincolorado.org

Center on Instruction (COI) (for ELLs)
  http://www.centeroninstruction.org/resources.cfm?category=ell

Center for Applied Linguistics (CAL)
  http://www.cal.org/topics/ell/

Classroom Instruction That Works with English Language Learners (Nebraska Department of Education)
  http://www.education.ne.gov/NATLORIGIN/Classroom_Instructions.html

Culturally Responsive Pedagogy and Practice National Center for Culturally Responsive Educational Systems (NCCRESt) (Arizona State University)
  http://www.nccrest.org/professional/culturally_responsive_pedagogy-and.html

Curriculum Based Readers Theatre Scripts
  http://www.rosalindflynn.com/EdThtrScripts.html

Developing Programs for English Language Learners: Introduction (Office of Civil Rights of U.S. Department of Education)
  http://www2.ed.gov/about/offices/list/ocr/ell/developing.html

Educating Students with Limited English Proficiency (LEP) and English Language Learners (ELL) (Pennsylvania Department of Education)
  http://www.education.state.pa.us/portal/server.pt/community/pa_codes/7501/ educating_students_with_limited_english_proficiency_(lep)_and_english_language_ learners_(ell)/507356

Education Week ELL Blog (also available via ¡Colorín Colorado!)
  http://blogs.edweek.org/edweek/learning-the-language/

Eliminating the Gaps, Language Acquisition Strategies for (Standard/Academic) English Language Learners (State of Washington, Office of Superintendent of Public Instruction [OSPI])
  http://www.k12.wa.us/CISL/EliminatingtheGaps/TeacherToolkit/Languageacquisiti onStrategies.aspx

English Language Learner (ELL) Program (Hawaii State Department of Education)
  http://doe.k12.hi.us/englishlanguagelearners/index.htm

English Language Learners (Arizona Department of Education)
  http://www.azed.gov/english-language-learners/

English Language Learners (Iowa Department of Education)
  http://educateiowa.gov/index.php?option=com_content&view=article&id=683&Itemi d=2789

English Language Learners (Maine Department of Education)
http://www.maine.gov/doe/special/ell.html

English Language Learners (ELL)(Missouri Department of Elementary and Secondary Education)
http://dese.mo.gov/qs/me/ell.htm

English Language Learners (Promising Practices) (Rhode Island Department of Education)
http://www.ride.ri.gov/applications/ell/

English Language Learners (The Education Alliance at Brown University)
http://www.alliance.brown.edu/ae_ells.php

English Language Learner Programs (Michigan Department of Education)
http://michigan.gov/mde/0,1607,7-140-6530_30334_40078---,00.html

English Language Learner Programs (North Dakota Department of Public Instruction)
http://www.dpi.state.nd.us/bilingul/index.shtm

English Language Learning (Illinois State Board of Education)
http://www.isbe.net/bilingual/

English Learners (EL) and English as a Second Language (ESL) Program (Kentucky Department of Education)
http://education.ky.gov/specialed/EL/Pages/default.aspx

English Learners (California Department of Education)
http://www.cde.ca.gov/sp/el/

English Learners (Minnesota Department of Education)
http://education.state.mn.us/MDE/JustParent/EngLearn/

English to Speakers of Other Languages (ESOL) and Title III. (Georgia Department of Education)
http://www.doe.k12.ga.us/Curriculum-Instruction-and-Assessment/Curriculum-and-Instruction/Pages/English-to-Speakers-of-Other-Languages-(ESOL)-and-Title-III.aspx

English to Speakers of Other Languages (ESOL) (Kansas State Department of Education)
http://www.ksde.org/Default.aspx?tabid=350

Engrish.com
http://www.engrish.com/most-popular/

ESOL/Title III (Maryland State Department of Education)
http://www.msde.maryland.gov/MSDE/programs/title_III/overview.htm

IEP and Instruction: English Language Learners (Virginia Department of Education)
http://www.doe.virginia.gov/special_ed/iep_instruct_svcs/english_lang_learners/index.shtml

LEP Links (Idaho State Department of Education)
http://www.sde.idaho.gov/site/lep/lep_links.htm

Limited English and Immigrant—Title III (Oregon Department of Education)
  http://www.ode.state.or.us/search/results/?id=106

Limited English Proficient (LEP) Students (Ohio Department of Education)
  http://education.ohio.gov/GD/Templates/Pages/ODE/ODEPrimary.aspx?page=2&To picID=499&TopicRelationID=499

Links of Interest to Students & Teachers of English as a Second Language
  http://iteslj.org/links

Literacy Resources for Learners of English as a Second Language (ESL/EFL) (The Literacy Web at the University of Connecticut)
  http://www.literacy.uconn.edu/eslhome.htm

Migration Information Source (Migration Policy Institute)
  http://www.migrationinformation.org/USfocus/

Multicultural Lesson Plans and Resources (Edmund Sass, Ed.D., Professor of Education, College of Saint Benedict/Saint John's University)
  http://www.cloudnet.com/~edrbsass/edmulticult.htm

Omniglot: The Online Encyclopedia of Writing Systems and Languages (A-Z index)
  http://www.omniglot.com/writing/index.htm

Professional Development: Teachers Repository (North Carolina Department of Public Instruction)
  http://www.ncpublicschools.org/profdev/repository/teachers/links?idNumber=4b

Programs & Services: English Language Learner (ELL) Programs (State of Vermont Department of Education)
  http://education.vermont.gov/new/html/pgm_esl.html

Reading and Writing for Critical Thinking International Consortium
  http://www.rwctic.org/

Reading and Writing Connections to Journey North
  http://www.learner.org/jnorth/tm/Lessons_RW.html

Rethinking Equity and Teaching for English Language Learners (RETELL) (Massachusetts Department of Elementary & Secondary Education)
  http://www.doe.mass.edu/retell/

Tapestry (videos and resources)
  http://tapestry.usf.edu

Teaching for Tolerance: ELL Best Practices Collection (Southern Poverty Law Center)
  http://www.tolerance.org/ell-best-practices-collection

Teachers of English to Speakers of Other Languages, Inc.
  http://www.tesol.org

Tenement Museum (preserves and interprets the history of immigration)
  http://www.tenement.org

Texas English Language Learners Portal (Texas Education Agency)
http://elltx.org/

Title III (Oklahoma State Department of Education)
http://www.ok.gov/sde/title-iii

Title III (Wyoming Department of Education)
http://edu.wyoming.gov/programs/federally_funded_programs/title_iii.aspx

Title III - English Language Acquisition (South Dakota Department of Education)
https://doe.sd.gov/oess/TitleIIIela.aspx

Title III Information (Bilingual Education and Foreign Language Studies of New York State Education Department)
http://www.p12.nysed.gov/biling/NEWTIII.html

Title III - Language Instruction for Limited-English Proficient and Immigrant Students (The Colorado Department of Education)
http://www.cde.state.co.us/FedPrograms/tiii/tiii.asp

Title III - Language Instruction for Limited-English Proficient and Immigrant Students (Indiana Department of Education)
http://www.doe.in.gov/achievement/english-learners/title-iii-language-instruction-limited-english-proficient-and-immigrant

Title III English as a Second Language: Language Instruction for Limited English Proficient and Immigrant Students (Tennessee Department of Education)
http://www.tn.gov/education/fedprog/fpesl.shtml

Title III, Language Instruction for Limited English Proficient Students, K-12 (New Hampshire Department of Education)
http://www.education.nh.gov/instruction/integrated/title_iii.htm

Title III, Part A - English Language Learners (Mississippi Department of Education)
http://www.mde.k12.ms.us/federal-programs/federal-programs---title-iii-ell

World-Class Instructional Design and Assessment (WIDA)
http://www.wida.us/

Videos

Coughlin, T., Coughlin, D., Krzycki, M., Documentary Educational Resources (Firm), & White Center Heights Elementary School. (2003). *A family of many nations.* Watertown, MA: Documentary Educational Resources.

Genie Presentation http://www.youtube.com/watch?v=bWzO8DtRd-s

Hagerman, C., & Rulfo, J. C. (Directors). (2009). *Los que se quedan (Those who remain).* Mexico City: Fundación BBVA Bancomer.

Pérez, T. A., Haynes, H., Open City Works (Firm), Canada Council for the Arts, National Geographic Television & Film, & Warner Home Video (Firm). (2007). *Wetback: The undocumented documentary*. Washington, D.C.: National Geographic.

Levien, R., & Widdershins Films. (2009). *Immersion*. San Francisco, CA: Widdershins Films.

TED Talk: *Patricia Kuhl, The Linguistic Genius of Babies*. http://www.ted.com/talks/patricia_kuhl_the_linguistic_genius_of_babies.html

You Talk Funny (and other opinions from AMERICAN TONGUES). http://www.youtube.com/watch?v=_vF9g37FCmk

INDEX